AT A THEATER NEAR YOU . . .

Harold Shaw Publishers
Wheaton, Illinois

The *Wheaton Literary Series*

Unless otherwise noted, Scripture quotations are taken from the *Holy Bible, New International Version*. Copyright © 1973, 1978, 1984 International Bible Society. Used by permission of Zondervan Publishing House. All rights reserved.

ISBN 0-87788-041-7

Library of Congress Cataloging-in-Publication Data

Patterson, Thomas, 1945-
    At a theater near you : screen entertainment from a Christian perspective / Thomas Patterson.
      p. cm. — (The Wheaton literary series)
    Includes bibliographical references.
    ISBN 0-87788-041-7 (pbk.)
    1. Motion pictures—Moral and ethical aspects. 2. Motion pictures—Religious aspects—Christianity. I. Title. II. Series.
PN1995.5.P33 1994
791.43′01′3—dc20   94-13363
                                                              CIP

---

99 98 97 96 95 94

10 9 8 7 6 5 4 3 2 1

To my mother and father

Contents

Acknowledgments

A lay person who ventures to write about any aspect of Christian life owes a debt to each of the pastors in his life. With this in mind I wish to pay tribute to the ministry of Dr. Thomas G. Cross, the late Dr. L. D. Johnson, the Rev. William Bouknight, and Dr. William T. Cherry. Bill Cherry and his wife, Ginny, represent the classic model of pastor and pastor's wife, and do so while remaining unique individuals. Their encouragement was essential to the planning and initiation of this project. The many other Christian teachers, preachers, and friends who have led and influenced my thinking will be impossible to name.

I wish to thank the staff of the Free Library of Philadelphia, and especially the courteous and enthusiastic crew in the Film and Video Department. A special debt of gratitude is owed to David Grossman, director of Film Forum Philadelphia and former director of Temple Cinematheque. He is one of those teachers whose love for his subject communicates irresistibly to others. His knowledge of our film heritage continues to be a source of information and inspiration.

Finally I must thank my wife, Ruth Ellen, without whose help I could never have written this book. Not only did she provide years of patient nurturing and moral support, but she also served as my first and best editor. I have relied on her intelligent evaluation page by page and chapter by chapter. Along with everything else, she was willing to sit through countless movies—some great, some not so great, and some pretty awful—without complaining, and always ready to share insights and reactions.

Introduction

My father is a warm, easygoing man who loves simple pleasures. He's also one of the finest Christians I have ever known. A self-acknowledged "country boy," he has never spent much money on commercial entertainment and never felt the least bit deprived on that account. He and my mother hardly ever go out to a movie, but, like everybody else, they enjoy watching television.

That is, they enjoy some of the television they watch. Hardly an evening goes by without Dad's ritual suggestion, "Let's see what's on TV tonight." But as often as not, at the end of a show he will offer the familiar plaintive response, "Why did I waste my time on that?"

Last year my parents finally bought a VCR. This gives them greater freedom in what they watch and offers an escape from TV's tiresome commercials. Dad will probably see more of the movies he likes to recall—"the kind they used to make," where the story was gripping but there was no confusion about who was good and who was bad, or which one was going to win. I hope he will find lots of these and enjoy them to his heart's content, but experience makes me cautious. I suspect that even with a VCR he will often end up saying, "Why did I waste my time on that?"

This book is an effort to deal with my dad's question as it applies to all of us. Why *do* we spend so many hours on entertainment that is unprofitable and unsatisfying? There are reasons—some good, some not so good. When they are added up, the conclusion is inescapable that we can do better. But how? The chapters to follow offer a number of simple suggestions.

In developing these proposals I attempt to evaluate both what is offered on the screen and the nature of our choices in viewing. The ideas involved have grown throughout years of reading, teaching, discussing, and, of course, watching. I have focused primarily on films, but with the conviction that most viewing is now done at home by way of movie channels or the VCR.

In recent years many of us have experienced a growing frustration over the state of popular culture. We have seen traditional standards sabotaged and traditional goals questioned or derided. The response of concerned people—Christians included—has been hesitant, confused, self-doubting. A controversy is stirred every few months by the release of a new movie or a new disc. There is a flurry of protest, and then the matter disappears. Maybe a new organization is formed to lobby Congress or rally public sentiment. This too disappears; it was formed to get our attention, and does, but the essence of a media society is that our attention moves on.

One of the great failings of the church in America is that it has not responded to the challenge of a media culture. The lack of coherence in our attitude reflects the lack of coherence in our understanding. (It is not a question of expertise in broadcasting. Televangelism and the electronic church may do more to complicate the problem than to solve it.) Christians have become viewers—like everyone else—but sometimes we have failed to see. We don't talk together about our media culture except to agree that we are often shocked and upset. We have not sat down together to analyze the impact various media have, the way they shape our attitudes and goals.

"It is the principal function of popular culture—though hardly its avowed purpose—to keep men from understanding what is happening to them."* Such is the blunt assessment of one modern writer. While we may not be quite so cynical, there is enough truth in his remark to start us thinking. The implications are too far-reaching to be ignored. If we consume TV and film fare naively, we are at the mercy of these media in knowing what to feel and what to value. Look at the role of television in politics for example: The process is not education, as some pretend, but a dangerous substitute for it. Education would equip us to use our electronic tools and toys without being captured by them.

Sooner or later America will begin to comprehend the nature of its media culture. We need somebody to take the lead. Christians today have

---

*William H. Gass, *Fiction and the Figures of Life,* Vintage Books (New York: Random House, Inc., 1972), 272.

an opportunity to assume this role, but we must begin by teaching ourselves.

We can counteract the "Why-did-I-waste-my-time-on-that?" syndrome. But we can only do so when we see our situation clearly, and when we are willing to think and talk about it. The world of screen entertainment offers incredible rewards if we learn to separate the gold from the dross. Until now we have failed to recognize that this separating takes continued, disciplined effort. And we have yet to discover how worthwhile the effort can be.

My hope for this book is that it will encourage such a discovery. It is meant not to provoke controversy but to invite discussion. If it can help Christians to do a little more thinking, a little more talking, about how we spend so much of our lives, it will serve its purpose well.

Chapter 1

The Guest Who
Took Over the House

When evening comes, you say, "It will be fair weather, for the sky is red," and in the morning, "Today it will be stormy, for the sky is red and overcast." You know how to interpret the appearance of the sky, but you cannot interpret the signs of the times.
Matthew 16:2-3

Some revolutions are over before we know they have started. Not the kind with guns and flags, but quiet background events that alter our lives just as surely, and even more profoundly. Sometimes we never fully comprehend what has happened—we just notice that things aren't the way they used to be. The transformation often stems from a technological development that puts us into a new relationship with our environment or with each other.

That is what has happened with the videocassette recorder. Following the introduction and spread of this invention, we have a different outlook on the world of movies and television. We are also forming a new set of habits in the use of leisure time. Our expectations in regard to commercial entertainment will never be the same.

The first VCR for home use was introduced by Sony in 1975. In 1980 about one million were in use. By 1990 the figure was up to 67 million, representing nearly 72 percent of television households.[1] In 1991 the VCR passed a milestone by appearing in three-fourths of *all* American homes.[2] Our embrace of this once-amazing invention has been so rapid that we already take it for granted. It goes right into our matrix of conveniences along with the telephone, the microwave, bank machines, and the rest.

The coming of the VCR has hardly caused the excitement that television did with its arrival. The use of videotape seems to be just a variation of TV viewing as we have always known it. But we may find more to be excited about with video than we first supposed. This book focuses on the VCR and the rewards that Christians will gain from a thoughtful approach to movies. However, since using a VCR also means watching TV, it is appropriate for us to consider at the outset our common experience of broadcast television.

The TV revolution was a 50s phenomenon, although television technology had been developed as early as the 1930s. It was only after the Second World War that TV sets became the ubiquitous commodity they were destined to be. Almost everyone reacted favorably back then. There were great expectations for the benefits society would reap. Visionary schemes for classroom television were greeted with enthusiasm. Some dreamed of a steady increase in literacy and cultural awareness among the underprivileged. If nothing else, we would all have at our fingertips hours of diverting entertainment each day and night.

Early TV broadcasting was rarely controversial; these were the Eisenhower years, and Americans were intent on enjoying the good life in a context that reaffirmed our traditional values. For what else had we fought and won the war? We could be silly; we could be sentimental; we could even engage in occasional concern about social problems. Television registered our ideological temperature with shows that ranged from "I Love Lucy" and "Howdy Doody" to "Playhouse 90."

It was the golden age of television; but like every golden age, this one couldn't last. Even by the end of the 50s, thoughtful people were beginning to voice disappointment and alarm. Most of the concern was over what was being broadcast, not the behavior of TV-watching itself. There were scandals involving big-money quiz shows; there was controversy over advertising for alcohol and tobacco products. We were dismayed to find that most of the laughter heard on our favorite comedies was "canned."

Finally there was a growing concern over television's impact on public affairs. This reached a peak after the 1960 presidential election, when the Nixon-Kennedy debates were considered a pivotal factor. The warning voices grew stronger and more numerous. Soon the phrase "vast wasteland" (as FCC chairman Newton Minnow characterized commercial programming) would be linked inseparably with television in the public mind.

After the Honeymoon

As television became widespread in other countries, some observers began to ponder the difference between our commercial system and the various European systems that are government sponsored. Our own Public Broadcasting System eventually appeared, with much fanfare and high hopes for the regeneration of American television. But public broadcasting, as much as it has to offer, commands less than a tenth of the average viewer's attention. And it has succeeded not at all in raising the level of commercial broadcasting. It took its place in our TV environment and now serves as a kind of window dressing to preserve the respectability of the medium.

Since the 60s, a steady stream of books and research projects focused on television. Children's viewing became the leading issue in the ongoing debate. Were our kids watching too much? Were they watching things that were not good for them? Was television undercutting other more important activities? The questions are still being asked. They are as troubling now, after years of careful research and analysis, as they ever were. But the emphasis on children often obscures questions about adults and television which are also important. We may have to realize that it's useless to evaluate children and TV without giving some attention to the viewing habits of the adults they live with.

There are many factors that make it hard for us to govern our children's television use. The single parent or the working mother can't easily say no to such an effective babysitter—it's too convenient to pass up. But this convenience comes at a price. Children view an average of thirty hours of television a week— four hours every night while Mom cooks dinner, and a couple on Saturday morning. And this is just the average. Imagine what it's like for children who watch a *lot* of television. How can we let them live this way? Doesn't it often start with the fact that we adults don't control our own TV intake?

We have what amounts to a national dependency, of children *and* adults. As in other forms of dependency, one of the signs is that we won't admit to it. Many of us even make a show of despising television. We like to use an assortment of derogatory nicknames for it, such as "idiot box" and "boob tube." At any gathering of Christians the conversation will turn sooner or later to how awful and worthless "the stuff on TV" is these days. And from the pulpit, how often do we get a random swipe at television in the course of a sermon? It's practically liturgical.

We gripe regularly about TV; then we come home each day and turn it on again. Can it be that we keep up our ritual of complaining just to placate conscience—to shelter our pride because down deep we think we're helpless to do anything?

All the while prophetic voices keep sounding in the wilderness. One after the other, scholars and researchers diagnose our television predicament for us. One after the other they are ignored. (People who attack television don't get a lot of free promotion on the talk shows.) Sad to say, Christians haven't paid any more attention than the rest of society.

Admittedly, some of the critics hurt their own cause by going to extremes. It's hard to take seriously a person who sees in television a scheme to undermine democracy, or a demonic assault on the nation's moral fiber. Even Newton Minnow's famous warning about the "vast wasteland" may have backfired; the phrase is remembered now as a quaint piece of trivia. We Americans don't much like a spoilsport, no matter what his credentials. Of course, if a majority ever did come to perceive television as a monster, it would be easier to organize an effective response. But TV isn't horrible or malevolent—it's easy and undemanding. That is one of the reasons we can't muster the energy to resist.

The Supersalesman
There are plenty of other reasons why we fail to control television and end up letting it control us instead. One of them is TV's unremitting campaign to sell us on itself. If everything else about television were still in doubt, there would be no question that it can sell. That's why advertisers keep coming back with bushels of money. Television ad expenditures went from nearly $3.6 billion in 1970 to over $28 billion in 1990.[3] Television is, more than anything else, an advertising medium.

When TV is not selling us the soaps and beverages and cars produced by sponsoring corporations, it's selling us itself. We are bombarded this hour with messages about what it wants us to see the next hour. It tells us tonight what it wants us to be doing tomorrow night. All of these appeals have a common element of pretense: that what we're being told to see is "important." The music, the graphics, the throbbing resonance of the voice-over, all assert the vast implications of the upcoming event.

In many ways TV news is just the same. Why else do we recognize a phrase like "details at eleven"? No one would want to do without television coverage of certain events—a presidential inauguration or a moon landing, for example. But TV news as a habit, which is what the networks strive mightily to impose, is overrated. If we simply want to be kept up-to-date, radio is far more efficient. If we want to understand, there is no comparison between a TV story and a newspaper or magazine article. The latter has a double advantage: adequate time for the reporter to present the material, and adequate time for us to absorb it—even if it means reviewing a sentence or paragraph.

Television networks and local stations make much over the way they keep us informed. Indeed, we are the most relentlessly informed population in history. But what difference has this made? It would be wonderful if TV news could produce an enlightened citizenry, eagerly involved in the democratic process. But alas, the evidence so far is not encouraging. What television produces is spectators.[4]

News has always been the cornerstone of television's respectability. People who would dismiss entertainment programming as worthless still cling to TV news as if it were sacred. The news has first claim on their time, no matter what claims children or spouse or their own tired bodies have. Thus the news functions as one of the strongest in television's array of hooks. The routine is familiar: "Let's just turn it on to get the news," or "I'm just watching so I can catch the news when this is over."

Television keeps selling us itself, and we keep buying. "Be there!" orders a network ad campaign, and we comply. Sportscasters assure us that this is a very important game, and we solemnly agree. How we want to believe! We're like the captain's daughter in *H.M.S. Pinafore*, when she is being courted by the First Lord of the Admiralty. As she explains to her father, "I know that he is truly a great and good man, for he told me so himself."

Most Americans, both Christian and non-Christian, have come to count on seeing television every day of their lives. But the dependence of our children is what is most obvious and alarming—our children, who are falling behind the rest of the world's young people in educational achievement. Unfortunately, even many experts now take a defeatist attitude in regard to children and television. They keep beating the drums for *better programming* because, after all, the kids are going to become addicted whatever we do.[5]

One expert who doesn't buy the assumption that TV is irresistible is Marie Winn, author of *The Plug-In Drug*. Winn challenges the notion that we need better programming because TV watching is inevitable. One chapter of her book reveals a stunning correlation between the rise of television and the decline of SAT scores among school children. The weight of the evidence and the force of her argument are devastating. *The Plug-In Drug* puts it plainly: Television requires control, not compromise.[6]

Meanwhile, the latest of many schemes to harness television for classroom use is the new school network, Channel One. This is an enterprise that offers schools "free" equipment if they agree to broadcast the network's programs and the commercials that accompany them. Channel One's promoters (and its apologists within the educational establishment) promise great benefits. But don't hold your breath. Asking a commercial television venture to rescue our schools is like putting Saddam Hussein in charge of a disarmament conference.

Ironically, no one has put the problem of children and television into focus better than Captain Kangaroo (Bob Keeshan). Speaking at a congressional hearing back in 1978, Keeshan labeled the amount of TV viewing by kids "a national crime." But he didn't blame the television industry. The ones responsible, he said, were the people who own the sets:

> The most often heard words in American homes today are not "I love you," . . . or "That was good, I like what you did there." I am afraid the most often spoken words in the American home today are, "I am busy. Go watch television."[7]

Keeshan added that whenever a parent decides to devote time to a child, "no television program on the face of the earth" can compete with the parent.

That was over fifteen years ago. The challenge of television in family life still confounds us. It is embarrassing—or should be—that the most cogent warnings come, not from our churches, but from dedicated researchers in the academic world. In his book *Go Watch TV!* Nat Rutstein quotes one such authority, Dr. David C. Jordan, director of the Center for the Study of Human Potential at the University of Massachusetts:

> I suspect that the most fundamentally damaging view of man that is perpetually emphasized on television is that he is a material being rather than a spiritual one.... The thesis presented by television is that having love is indeed desirable, and you can get it by using the right cosmetics, the right hair sprays . . . wash your clothes with the most powerful detergents, ad infinitum, and you will become lovable and will therefore be loved. Love is thus made dependent upon commercially available material things. It is difficult to imagine a greater distortion of a truth so basic to our sanity.[8]

When I read these words I am reminded of that urgent appeal of Paul to the Christians at Rome: "Do not conform any longer to the pattern of this world, but be transformed by the renewing of your mind. Then you will be able to test and approve what God's will is—his good, pleasing and perfect will" (Romans 12:2). This verse has always stood out in bold relief as a guideline for Christian living. The image that J. B. Phillips hit upon in translating it is especially effective: "Don't let the world around you squeeze you into its own mold." But the whole thrust of commercial television is to do just that.

In too many homes television has been like a clever, fun-loving house guest who was welcomed with great excitement. He delighted us initially with his jokes and stories, but at the same time he was exerting more and more influence over what we did and thought. Without our realizing it, he was taking over the house.

We couldn't have a meal until it suited The Guest, and then he would monopolize the conversation. He wouldn't let our kids do their homework or get the sleep and exercise they needed. Reading he absolutely refused to allow. Meaningful conversation—between, say, husband and wife—was out. And now the stories are stale, the jokes utterly predictable, but The Guest stays on.[9]

Well, we may still love the guy, but it's time to get him in line . . . or show him the door.

Notes to Chapter 1

1. U.S. Bureau of the Census, *Statistical Abstract of the United States: 1993* (113th edition.) Washington, D.C., 1993, 561.

2. Andy Wickstrom, "VCRs bucked the trend to post a sales increase in '91," *Philadelphia Inquirer,* 12 March 1992, sec. C, p. 10.

3. U.S. Bureau of the Census, *Statistical Abstract of the United States: 1992* (112th edition.) Washington, D.C., 1992, 559.

4. For an excellent evaluation of the news phenomenon, see Neil Postman, *Amusing Ourselves to Death: Public Discourse in the Age of Show Business* (New York: Penguin Books, 1986), 6–10.

5. See remarks of Peggy Charren, former head of Action for Children's Television, quoted in "Catchy videos have tots singing—and learning," *USA Today,* 28 April 1988, sec D, p. 4.

6. Marie Winn, *The Plug-In Drug: Television, Children and the Family,* revised ed. (New York: Penguin Books, 1985), 82–83.

7. White House Conference on Families, 1978, *Joint Hearings Before the Subcommittee on Child and Human Development, U.S. Senate and the Subcommittee on Select Education, House of Representatives* (Washington, D.C.: Government Printing Office, 1978), 706.

8. Letter to the author, quoted in Nat Rutstein, *Go Watch TV!* (New York: Sheed and Ward, Inc., 1974), 112.

9. For an account drawn from real life, see Colman McCarthy, "Ousting the Stranger from the House," *Newsweek,* 25 March 1974, quoted in Winn, 262–263.

DENNIS THE MENACE

"WHICH CAME FIRST, DAD, TOYS OR CARTOONS?"

Chapter 2

Escape from
the Wasteland

Good Will: An open door is set before thee, and no man can shut it.
Christian: Now I begin to reap the benefits of my hazards.
Good Will: But how is it that you came alone?
Christian: Because none of my Neighbors saw their danger as I saw mine.
John Bunyan, *The Pilgrim's Progress*

We live in an age when Christian values are under intense and unremitting pressure. Earlier generations could count on most of society's institutions to reinforce those values—the school, the arts, even government if we go back far enough. But our world is not like it was in 1909, when the mayor of New York revoked the licenses of all the movie houses in the city for violations of the Sunday closing law. (His action didn't stand in the courts even then.) Now, one after the other, those reinforcing elements have been "taken out of the game." At the same time the pressures on young people are proportionally greater, as so much of our cultural/entertainment product is targeted at them.

In this changed environment, many Christians are coming to see that child rearing and family life are now the front lines of the faith. We are commissioned as ever to preach and teach the gospel. But when we must address a plugged-in world that thinks it has heard everything, the responsibility of *living* the gospel becomes ever more pressing. We have to show as well as tell. And the living is grounded in the Christian home.

The foundations of Christian theology are linked inseparably with the concept of a loving, sustaining relationship between parent and child (see

Romans 8 or Galatians 4). This is fundamental to our understanding of the Incarnation. Over and over again our Bible gives us vivid examples of parental love, and of reciprocal loyalty from children to parents. It goes from century to century, from Abraham and Isaac to Eunice and Timothy (not forgetting Grandmother Lois). Our faith is something that is given to us out of love, that lives in love.

The basic laboratory where we discover, study, and practice love is the family. This is why we find the theme so often in the teaching of Jesus. Perhaps it is why we sense a special depth of compassion in such acts as the raising of the widow's son (Luke 7:13) or of Jairus's daughter. It is what gives the story of the Prodigal Son its remarkable power. It is even implied in that beloved scene of the Savior placing a child beside him as he clears up the nonsense over "who is the greatest in the kingdom of heaven."

In an age that challenges Christianity as much as any since the days of the Romans, the family must be maintained as the crucible of faith. It is up to us to make it work, not only for our own children's sake, but for the world outside as well. We are the light of the world, we've been told in no uncertain terms. We need not duck our head and look somewhere else.

In our struggle to maintain the family, television looms as a factor we can no longer ignore. Nor can we afford to kid ourselves about the power it holds over us. Getting TV under control will take a lot more than good intentions. It will take work—at understanding causes and effects, and developing successful plans of action. But the problem is so far-reaching that it demands greater resources of knowledge and discipline than most of us can muster on our own. To meet this challenge we must find a power that is beyond us, and that is strong enough to resist the media siege we are under.

Allies for the Asking

Fortunately, Christians have access to such a power. It can be found in our personal faith; it can be shared in our churches and Sunday schools. Until now, however, churches have been slow to recognize and address the challenge of a media society, and television in particular. In order for Christian parents to win the struggle, this has to change.

I don't mean to suggest that we ask Sunday school teachers and youth leaders to do *our* job of guiding children. Rather, I propose that we exploit the resource of our adult groups so that parents can help each other master the challenge of television. The effects of TV could be taken up in Sunday evening classes, special groups meeting in homes, even regular Sunday school sessions if necessary. Small groups within a church have always featured mutual encouragement through the sharing of experiences. The Christian church invented the "support group" long before twentieth-century psychologists stumbled onto it. "Carry each other's burdens," Paul wrote, "and in this way you will fulfill the law of Christ" (Galatians 6:2).

The concerned group—whether formed for the purpose or already in place—could start by reading and discussing some of the important books that have explored the television problem. The list that follows this chapter may be helpful; however, it is certainly not exhaustive. Group members will want to draw on more than one source as they prayerfully consider a plan of action. For my money, Marie Winn's *The Plug-In Drug* should head any list. It deserves to be read thoughtfully by every Christian parent in America. It is scrupulously researched, and Winn writes with never-failing common sense.

I don't believe there is time for any of us to sniff at the idea of studying a secular source. It would be irresponsible to neglect the help of the best, most knowledgeable advisors. As the Old Testament writer put it, "Make plans by seeking advice; if you wage war, obtain guidance" (Proverbs 20:18).

Our churches need to get better at guiding parents in their incredibly demanding job. It will take more than scheduling a once-a-year workshop with a "guest star" from the field of Christian counseling. It will take more than repeated calls for home discipline from the pulpit. Christian parenting demands highly developed skills and greater wisdom than most of us possess as individuals. The first priority is to establish prayerful group consideration of the nuts-and-bolts challenges of parenting.

In the context of our adult groups, we need God's grace to make us honest and help us put away our fear of admitting inadequacy. Sometimes this can be harder in a church community than anywhere else. Where are we more stubborn about looking like we know what we're doing than with our kids? But this is something the Bible tells us with utter clarity: We've got to make our inadequacy the *starting point* in order to receive God's power. If we will do this, the burdens of parenthood can be shared in the spirit of Galatians 6:2—and so can the joys!

If Christian parents learned to work together in mastering their problems, our homes would be a light source for the nation. Controlling television could be a breakthrough endeavor. Suppose a group of parents, after careful study of the evidence and consideration of their own experience, decides to make an effort for change. If it appears that TV time should be limited to a certain number of hours, the group could make this commitment together. Members could continue to offer each other encouragement, counsel, and prayer as they strive to meet their goals.

If this kind of practical support is too much to expect from our church, where should we look? "You are the salt of the earth," Jesus said. "But if the salt loses its saltiness, how can it be made salty again? It is no longer good for anything, except to be thrown out and trampled by men" (Matthew 5:13).

The Impact of the VCR
As all-pervasive as television has become, we are yet in the midst of drastic changes in its use. Pay-per-view, HDTV, and interactive television will doubtless have repercussions that no one can predict. As TV technology grows more dazzling, it will present new problems and dilemmas. However, those who accept the challenge of controlling television have an important resource in the VCR.

Since the early 1970s, pollster Louis Harris has conducted a series of surveys focusing on how people use their leisure time. The studies provide vital information to cultural organizations, particularly those in the performing arts. To no one's surprise, these surveys indicate that the amount of leisure time keeps going down (from 26.2 hours a week in 1973 to 16.6 hours a week in 1987). At the same time, attendance at live cultural events such as opera and concerts has also decreased.[1]

In charting these trends, Harris has noted a significant development: Those people whose leisure time is shrinking the most are the ones most likely to own a VCR. "There is a reason why the VCR is becoming a key instrument in the time-short era into which this country has now entered," Harris observes. "People want to be able to pick and choose precisely what they will be doing with their precious but limited time."[2] The VCR seems destined to become ever more important to the cultural life of America.

Most of us have long since accepted the bond with television. Typically there is not just one family set, but multiple sets around the house. In many homes there is a set for every person. It remains to be seen whether, or how quickly, the VCR will spread to multiple locations. There may be a positive effect in the fact that the video machine is coupled to the family's largest, "central" TV set. Being all together, whatever we are watching, often yields unexpected rewards.

Many people use the VCR primarily as an aid to television viewing. They use the automatic timing device to record a favorite program, or they have another family member tape a show while watching it. The ultimate value of this practice depends on the choice of what is taped. But one element in play here is entirely positive. When a person sits down to watch a television show that was taped earlier, he or she is exercising more initiative and judgment than the person who merely sits down to see what's on.

This wholesome element of choice also sets video rentals apart from TV viewing. Thus we come to the second major use of the VCR. For many of us, the viewing of feature films at home is the most important benefit offered by the new device.

There was a time not long ago when the American movie industry viewed the VCR with unmixed dread. Some people envisioned the doom of the traditional movie theater. But after a relatively brief legal shootout, the movie rental business won a firm position in the marketplace, and the movie industry learned to live with its new in-law quite happily. In the best "If-you-can't-lick-'em, join-'em" tradition, the movie companies found ways to exploit the video trade for good old-fashioned profits. Rather than closing down the theaters, video may actually be increasing the national diet of movies.

The advantages of viewing films at home are obvious. Mere convenience is a powerful factor, of course, and running a close second is economics. Renting a movie for two or three dollars is a lot cheaper than paying five or six per person at the theater. Even more important may be the time and trouble of driving and finding a place to park. These considerations are important to different age groups for different reasons.

For teenagers, a VCR in the home alters viewing habits drastically. The low cost is a major factor; almost as important are the abundance of available titles and the total informality of the experience. For young adults, whether married or single, the inducements may be even greater. The VCR provides a quick and easy form of entertainment for dates or for groups of friends. And for young parents it is an alternative far and away more appealing than paying a babysitter and wondering about the children all evening.

For all audiences the proliferation of outlets is a major advantage. More and more rental stores have appeared in urban and suburban locations. If you don't feel like making a trip to the video store, you can even pick up your movie at the supermarket. For cable-TV customers the dial-a-video plan may be just around the corner. This would be the ultimate in convenience, if not economy.

More Possibilities, More Pitfalls

While the VCR will increase dramatically the number of movies a family is likely to see, another effect may be just as significant. Those young people who watch two and three films per weekend do so in many cases with a minimum of supervision. Given the natural curiosity of youth, the choices may vary widely—from innocuous to highly questionable fare. If a teenager brings home a movie charged with eroticism and immorality, it may not be from a conscious desire to view shocking films. Likewise, it doesn't necessarily indicate a permissive or negligent attitude in Christian parents.

What I am referring to is not conspiracy on the one hand or cop-out on the other, but merely habit. The teens come home with the movies on Saturday. They announce titles to whoever wants to know. Dad takes another dip with his paintbrush, and Mom nods absently over the clothes basket. One movie goes by in the afternoon. A second starts rolling at 10:30, when Mom and Dad are too tired to stay awake and watch. By Monday the young minds of their children have logged in several hours of Hollywood product. The product has been consumed with no "quality control" whatsoever—no value judgment made or attempted—because parents were not paying attention and children were not equipped to try.

Mom and Dad often get a better idea after the fact what kind of viewing their teenage children have done. That is when you hear the familiar cry, "I didn't know it was *that* kind of movie!" But teenagers are notoriously immune to hand-wringing and belated warnings. It is too late when the tapes have already gone back to the store. What is worse, parents who find themselves unable to influence their children's choices often fall into a ritual of ineffective carping just to salve their own consciences. The young always know where to file that kind of input.

The VCR is not only opening up new and troubling horizons for young people. Adult Christians would do well to examine their changing movie habits also. The adult VCR owner is probably watching more movies than before, and like the youngsters, he or she is likely to be sampling *more kinds* of movies as well. Christians who never made it to the mall theater for anything but a Walt Disney feature or *The Sound of Music* now come home from the video store with films of all kinds.

The reasons for this new variety are natural. We've all had the experience of going to pick up a particular title and finding it already out. That throws the vote open, and we end up browsing the shelves for ten minutes, waiting for another title to jump out at us. We are now vulnerable to a number of random factors. By chance we may glimpse something we remember wanting to see. We may be led to pull one box off the shelf because it shows a picture of a performer we like, or believe we like. We may go up and down the aisle looking for something similar to our first choice (the one that is out) because we're in the mood for that type of story, be it comedy, suspense, or whatever.

Operating over all these possible influences is the unconscious command to ourselves that we must find *something* to watch. After all, we have gone to this much trouble to come to the store—we can't let the trip go to waste. We cannot accept failure. So we end up watching and having in our homes movies that got there by chance, chosen (if that is the word) almost at random. When this happens, we are dangerously close to the "Why-did-I-waste-my-time-on-that?" syndrome.

Redeeming the Time

Sometimes we fail to find what we wanted at the video store and instead come home with something better. This is a fine thing, and if it appeals to someone's gambling instinct, he or she will be pleased to attempt it repeatedly. The idea of taking a tiny leap into the unknown and finding an unexpected prize has universal appeal. In this case it is enhanced because nothing very important is at risk—just a couple of hours' time.

But Christians do well to avoid gambling, even if it is time they would play with. The throwing away of time is as serious for a Christian as the loss of any other resource. As Paul advised the saints at Ephesus, "Be very careful, then, how you live—not as unwise but as wise, making the most of every opportunity, because the days are evil" (Ephesians 5:15-16). In the King James translation of this passage, the key phrase is "redeeming the time." It expresses a principle that is important throughout the Bible.

Now this is a pretty old-fashioned idea, but it is one of the basic assumptions of this book. The Christian must always make it a goal to use his or her time profitably. The secular world of the 90s has pretty much standardized another system. There is time devoted to work. It *matters* what we do then, because the boss or the client is watching and money is at stake. Then there is time off from work. What we do then *doesn't* matter, except that we please ourselves as much as possible. Squeezed awkwardly into this second area is something known in current jargon as "quality time," which we are supposed to ration out to children and other loved ones who need us.

Certainly the efforts to promote quality time with family are well meant and deserve encouragement. But for Christians, there is not time that counts and time that does not count. There is not quality time and whatever is the opposite. For when we are redeemed by God's reconciling love in Christ, *all* our time is quality time. We move over into the realm that Paul explored for us, saying that for him to live is Christ. Or, as he explained to the Romans, "None of us lives to himself alone and none of us dies to himself alone. If we live, we live to the Lord" (Romans 14:7-8).

So what does this have to do with television and movies? In our zeal for Christ, are we to eliminate all forms of entertainment and relaxation, making ourselves dedicated drudges? I believe not. We may picture Paul or certain other heroic Christians—John Wesley, Hudson Taylor, Tom Dooley—as persons who never had time to laugh or be at ease. But this is largely a myth of our own making. In Paul's letters, one thing that stands out is his warm regard for various individual friends. Considering such genuine affection, it is hard to imagine that there were not some high good times shared in the homes of the faithful. The joyless zealot is to be found serving other causes than the cause of Christ.

If we are honest with ourselves, we all recognize our creaturely need for relief from the cares of life. The fact is, for most of us leisure time is not really an option. We have to have it in order to keep functioning. In the context of using our time well, including leisure time, there is a place for television, for movies, and for the VCR. There is even something to be said for the fun of browsing in a video store. The purpose of this book is essentially to make all of these experiences better.

Our primary concern from here on will be with films, for a number of reasons. Their accessibility and their variety are major considerations. Just as important is the way they lend themselves to free choice—to the discrimination of the individual. This book has been written to help the Christian viewer locate and appreciate rewarding films, whether on cable TV, on videotape, or in the theater.

The best way to escape the wasteland of commercial television is to find something better. With the right preparation and approach, Christians can enhance not only their viewing enjoyment but even the experience of selecting a film or reading a movie review. We can proceed confidently in the spirit of Philippians 4:8, and "if anything is excellent or praiseworthy," we can enjoy it—even on the silver screen.

Notes to Chapter 2

1. Rick Lyman, "Attendance at arts events declines, "*Philadelphia Inquirer,* 16 March 1988, Sec. A, p. 1.

2. *Ibid.*

Suggested Sources for Group Study of Children and Television

Kelley, Michael R. *A Parent's Guide to Television: Making the Most of It.* New York: John Wiley & Sons, 1983.

Moody, Kate. *Growing Up on Television: A Report to Parents.* New York: McGraw-Hill, 1984.

Rutstein, Nat. *Go Watch TV!* New York: Sheed and Ward, 1974.

Schrag, Robert L. *Taming the Wild Tube: A Family's Guide to Television and Video.* Chapel Hill: The University of North Carolina Press, 1990.

Schultze, Quentin J. *Redeeming Television: How TV Changes Christians—How Christians Can Change TV.* Downers Grove, Illinois: InterVarsity Press, 1992.

Schwarz, Meg, ed. *TV & Teens: Experts Look at the Issues.* Reading, Massachusetts: Addison-Wesley, 1982. (Published by Action for Children's Television.)

Wilkins, Joan Anderson. *Breaking the TV Habit.* New York: Charles Scribner's Sons, 1982.

Winn, Marie. *The Plug-In Drug: Television, Children & the Family.* Revised edition. New York: Penguin Books, 1985.

Winn, Marie. *Unplugging the Plug-In Drug: Help Your Children Kick the TV Habit.* New York: Penguin Books, 1987.

"The Monday movie will be back after the messages
that follow the following messages."

Chapter 3

If Shakespeare
Were Alive Today

The eye is the lamp of the body. If your eyes are good, your whole body will be full of light. But if your eyes are bad, your whole body will be full of darkness.
Matthew 6:22-23

Like everyone else, Christians need relaxation to remain healthy in body, mind, and spirit. Of course there are lots of ways to unwind, and many of them do not require entertainment—certainly not entertainment that is packaged and sold commercially. The best kinds of relaxation don't involve spending money at all. This needs to be acknowledged plainly in a book about movies and television.

We must have no illusions about the value of media entertainment. To a great extent it is limited by its very nature. For example, compare watching a film to an evening of informal fellowship with friends. Both experiences offer the benefit of relaxation and the easing of work-related tensions. But interactive companionship has the advantage of fostering and strengthening the bonds between persons—a result not found in any spectator experience.

The good fellowship that we associate with the sharing of food and drink has been honored in every age and culture. It occurs in straw huts and stone cottages, log cabins and palaces. In the West we have developed special settings as diverse as the Bavarian beer garden and the American church picnic. They differ radically in the nature and outlook of the participants, but they share a potential for the expression, however commonplace, of love for one's neighbor.

With all its virtues, the practice of gathering together for fellowship can also become a joyless ritual. The deceptive aspect of revelry has been known since the beginning of history, but there are those in each generation who have to learn the hard way. Bars and night clubs have a central place in today's highly mobile youth culture. Even high-school students flock to clubs in imitation of their elders. For some of them the biggest challenge in life seems to be how to beat the age restriction for alcohol, or how to avoid getting "carded." Adult Christians, especially the parents of teenagers, may well be concerned about the spending of time and money in this fashion.

For Christian young people the most viable alternative to partying is often commercial entertainment. There can hardly be a church activity planned for them every night of the week, or every weekend during school term. It is doubtful whether such an exclusive social agenda would be wise in any case. We can be thankful that there are other worthwhile options. And just as they have done for so many years, movies head the list. It follows that one of the best things we can do for the young is to teach them how to recognize and value the best in movies.

An Art Form for Everybody

It isn't hard to see how movies have remained for so long the most popular form of commercial entertainment. From the very beginning they were a pastime of the common people; as such they were often derided by the well-to-do and the more sophisticated. The experience of the moving image was so compelling that movies were not dependent on a verbal element to succeed. The level of literacy or "culture" of the audience was irrelevant.

Thus the earliest movies, around the turn of the century, were ideal entertainment for the growing population of America's cities. At the same time they performed an important educational function. In his early survey, *The Rise of the American Film*, Lewis Jacobs explained,

Besides offering a social occasion and an emotional experience, they supplied audiences with information and ideas. Immigration was at its peak in 1902–1903, and the movies gave the newcomers, particularly, a respect for American law and order, an understanding of civic organizations, pride in citizenship and in the American commonwealth. . . . More vividly than any other single agency they revealed the social topography of America to the immigrant, to the poor, and to the country folk.[1]

Of course the patrons of 1903 didn't go to the movies to be educated or civilized; they went to have a good time. The same is true of us today. But between 1900 and 1920 a profound change took place in the way moving pictures were created and the way they were perceived. In this transformation movies went from being a mere novelty, an arcade attraction, to something that would eventually qualify as an art form.

The filmmakers learned to tell a story, not just present a scene or an event. And they learned to tell the story in ways that were peculiar to the medium of film, taking the audience from one part of the action to another in the blink of an eye, drawing them suddenly close to fill the screen with an important detail (a trembling hand, a concealed gun) or providing a long shot with a broad sweep of scenery.

The precedent-setting achievement in America was *The Great Train Robbery*, made in 1903 by Edwin S. Porter. This movie was greeted with such enthusiasm that other filmmakers around the world were soon busy turning out imitations. By developing the narrative possibilities of the new medium, Porter and his imitators nudged the movies closer to the circle of art forms such as the play, the novel, and the ballet, which had long since established their respectability.

There is prophetic significance in the subject that Porter chose for his landmark feature. Quaint as it may seem now, *The Great Train Robbery* was timely in its day; that sort of crime was all too common in the West, and much reported in the newspapers. Movies were to keep as their principal domain the world of realistic action, of danger introduced into the lives of ordinary people, and of rough, inevitable justice. Many of the best and most successful movies offer a vivid depiction of everyday life, revealing in turn its sweetness, its sadness, quite often its ugliness, but also its moments of splendor.

Movies still hold a questionable tenure among the established arts. Nevertheless, filmmakers over the years have discovered a significant number of things movies can achieve that can't be done in any other medium. Neither live theater nor books can match the movies for physical scope; for swiftness of pace; for the integration of music, color, and light;

for verisimilitude in representing reality. This is not to depreciate the other arts, but simply to underline the differences.

From one decade to the next, movies maintain the promise of excitement, spectacle, and adventure. Each decade brings forth new artists who strive to wring from the medium still better results. The roll call goes from D. W. Griffith (the first great American master) through names like Capra, Disney, Hitchcock, and Lean, to contemporary figures such as Spielberg and Lynch.

The great movies are popular in every sense of the word, and we have reached a point where we can see that they are also enduring classics of our culture. It used to be a common remark when I was in school that "if Shakespeare were alive today, he would be making movies." I seem to recall that it always came up when someone was trying to get out of doing a book report! But there is a piquant trace of truth in the remark. Of all our media and arts, movies are probably the most alive—the most responsive to our society in its constant changes. And the artistic potential of movies has never been fully explored, even now.

The Threat and the Promise
Like every other powerful invention of humanity, movies have always offered dual possibilities—wholesome or harmful. Even before 1910, while movies were educating the immigrants and the illiterate, some filmmakers were introducing salacious material into their productions. The practice was soon curbed, but it has returned with much greater impact in later decades.

Unfortunately, movies could reproduce unwholesome experience quite as vividly as the harmless and the uplifting. The enhanced impression of reality, the indelible impact of the magnified image, quickly gave alarm to the cautious. Screen historian Arthur Knight cites the first screen kiss as a case in point. It occurred in a standard short of the early period—one of Edison's Kinetoscopes—and was taken from an already well-known play. Comparing the impact of film with that of stage performance, Knight comments,

> This difference between stage and screen is perhaps best pointed up in the popular *May Irwin-John C. Rice Kiss* (1896), a scene from the play, *The Widow Jones*. Its few moments of magnified osculation resulted in

the first scandalized attempt at film censorship. The "kiss" may have been harmless enough in the [live] theater, but seen in full close-up it suddenly became so much more "real."[2]

The power of film to create an immediate emotional impact is probably what sets it off most clearly from other arts. Motion pictures can both show and tell. Pictorial art has always had the capability of presenting an image so vivid that with only a moment's glimpse the viewer may carry the memory for a lifetime. The movies bring to this phenomenon a giant scale, and multiply the potential with their ability to link images consecutively. The visual experience is heightened by lens and lighting effects. To this is added the verbal dimension in dialog and occasional narration. The aural frame is further filled with natural background sound. And beyond all this there is the addition of music at key points to intensify the emotional impact of the whole.

One thing is clear about the movie experience: Its effects can be achieved with very little effort on the part of the viewer. With all of these sensory impressions coming at us from the screen and the sound system, we just need to sit there and let it happen to us. When this is compared to the reading of a book or even the viewing of a live drama, the contrast is greater than we often suspect.

In live performances we have the visual language of the actor with its resources of gesture, attitude, look, etc. But we take in these statements with no assistance from a substitute eye (like the camera) that concentrates or expands our frame, brings near or withdraws the subject from us. Scenic effects almost always need the total commitment of our own imagination to succeed. And a high pitch of mental energy is required in order for us to stay in the flow of dialog. Moreover, to follow the thought of a character we must depend entirely on ourselves and the actor—there will be no cut to a far-off location that occupies the hero's thoughts, no fade-in on a scene recalled from the past.

We probably compare films to novels more often than to live drama. Anyone who has been disappointed with the movie version of a favorite novel knows something of the possible differences. (We should also recognize that some stories come off better in movie form than they are originally in the book.) The novel generally demands a higher level of imaginative effort than a stage play. Continuous concentration is needed for us to follow the story and to keep the characters fixed in our minds. Whatever mental images we see of the events recounted we must create with our own imaginations, guided by the skill of the writer.

The movies are so successful and so popular, in a sense, because we don't have to do as much to enjoy them. All of the images are ready-made. The movies allow us to be lazy. But we need not confine ourselves to a negative assessment. This capability of film to reach across the frontiers of our senses can be a remarkable blessing. Children are enabled to visualize the world in aspects that would be impossible otherwise. Those of us who lack a great imaginative gift, or those who for whatever reason are not skilled readers, can all be grateful for the "magic" of film. The movies offer everyone a prime avenue of escape from the stresses and anxieties of life. While any form of escapism must be employed with restraint, a good film offers us an interval of release that is altogether harmless and wholesome.

But movies offer much more than mere escape. All of us, no matter how literate or how familiar with the arts, can use film to tap into experiences of remarkable intensity and value if we choose to—that is, if we come to the movies ready to put our mind and imagination to work just as energetically as when we read a book.

Some of the most important passages in the Bible report the direct encounters of Old Testament heroes with God. In these incidents it is made clear that the visual apprehension of the Almighty would be the ultimate human experience. The effect was so overwhelming that men had to be shielded from it, as was Moses on Mount Sinai (see Exodus 33). Isaiah felt such alarm after his vision of the Lord that he cried, "Woe to me. . . . For I am a man of unclean lips, and I live among a people of unclean lips, and my eyes have seen the King, the LORD Almighty" (Isaiah 6:5).

In both the Old and New Testaments, the dramatic healing of the blind reminds us of the importance of vision. The idea is reinforced by the warnings directed toward those who have eyes but cannot see (Isaiah 6:10, Jeremiah 5:21, Mark 8:18). The inestimable value of seeing and the power of the visual image are reflected throughout the Scriptures. With this in mind, perhaps we can consider more seriously an art that is based on the creation of visions.

Since motion pictures are capable of doing so much so well, it is sad that they have ever been misused. But that is clearly the case, and the history of movies in America is a chronology of recurring controversy over moral issues. In the chapter to follow, we shall take a brief look at this fascinating and frustrating record.

Notes to Chapter 3

1. Lewis Jacobs, *The Rise of the American Film: A Critical History* (New York: Harcourt, Brace, 1939; reprint, New York: Teachers College Press, 1968), 12.

2. Arthur Knight, *The Liveliest Art*, revised ed. (New York: New American Library, 1979), 13.

Chapter 4

The Good, the Pure,
and the Profitable

For you were once darkness, but now you are light in the Lord. Live as children of light (for the fruit of the light consists in all goodness, righteousness and truth) and find out what pleases the Lord.
Ephesians 5:8-10

On December 23, 1908, there was a public hearing at City Hall in New York. The atmosphere was tense. In the aldermanic chamber, where Mayor George McClellan presided, the gallery was packed. People waited to vent the anger and alarm they had been storing for months. It was time for a showdown on the moving picture issue.

The mayor had called this meeting to obtain information and guidance in the matter of Sunday showings. To no one's surprise the debate soon extended much further, covering the general impact of movies on society. Clergymen from almost every denomination rose to speak out against the theaters, while movie producers and exhibitors countered with a spirited defense of their rights. At the heart of the debate was the effect of movies on young people. The Reverend Dr. J. M. Foster no doubt spoke for many when he said,

> Is a man at liberty to make money from the morals of people? Is he to profit from the corruption of the minds of children? The man who profits from such things is doomed to double damnation.[1]

The meeting went on for more than four hours. Before it was over, the movie men came to realize that they were fighting for their existence.

The next day, December 24, Mayor McClellan issued an order that revoked the license of every moving picture show in the city. It meant the shutting down of about 550 movie houses.

This was the first pitched battle on the frontier of movie morality. From that day on, the problem has never really gone away. Friction between the movie industry and various champions of morality has continued to produce public drama like that New York controversy. We find a repeating cycle in which public concern rises to a peak every ten or fifteen years, and the movie industry responds with some sort of conciliatory action. Besides the conflict of 1908, there were significant crises or turning points in 1922, 1934, and the late 60s. In each case the industry took voluntary action to protect profits from the damage threatened by moral activists.

It is tempting to dismiss these Hollywood compromises as self-serving and hypocritical, but we should consider the evidence carefully before passing judgment. The people in the movie business have always been in it to make money—the same reason people are in most other businesses. And those who succeed in making money are admired in our society, perhaps more than anywhere else in the world. If Americans attach so much prestige to profits, we can hardly be surprised when businessmen act on the principle that the end justifies the means.

This chapter will focus on the evils and excesses of the movie world, as well as the efforts made through the years to combat them.

The Sources of Conflict

The first decade of this century was the heyday of the nickelodeon. In cities and towns all across America, vacant stores or offices were being turned into quickie movie halls by blocking out the light and crowding in as many rows of chairs as possible. There were nicer showplaces, where patrons might be charged as much as fifteen cents, but the masses were able to get into the new screening rooms for a nickel. It gave them a show of about twenty minutes' duration. The public appetite for this new attraction was virtually insatiable.

The spread of the nickelodeons was followed in short order by a wave of concern among church and civic leaders. All sorts of objections were raised, ranging from the danger of fire in the crowded halls to the moral impact of the films themselves. According to *Harper's Weekly*, the police commissioner of New York "denounced the nickel madness as pernicious, demoralizing, and a direct menace to the young."[2]

The situation in New York City in the winter of 1908–1909 reveals a number of the conflicting forces at work. Opposition to the nickelodeons was concentrated in churches and civic organizations, but soon this sentiment became strong enough to claim the attention of the politicians. The issue of Sunday showings brought the movie industry into direct conflict with law and morality. On one side stood theater owners, who made much of their income from the working class on Sundays. On the other side were churches and political leaders who sought to defend the Sabbath against the desecration of money-hungry showmen.

When Mayor McClellan shut down the nickelodeons, there were two reasons cited: first, a widespread concern about fire safety; and second, the moral concern regarding Sunday shows. According to the mayor's decree, every theater was to be given a thorough reinspection for safety before a new license would be granted. Furthermore, licenses would only be issued to those who agreed in writing not to operate the shows on Sunday.[3] Movie officials immediately went to court to fight back, and they succeeded in having the mayor's order overturned. It had been far too sweeping to meet the requirements of the law.

In making their case, industry spokesmen offered a number of conciliatory proposals. They had already agreed at the mayor's hearing to accept censorship. Now they promised to correct deficiencies in safety as well. Most important, the movie faction lost no time in focusing on the economic aspect of the problem. The industry had grown so fast, they contended, that there were now thousands in New York alone who depended on it for their jobs. If allowed to stand, Mayor McClellan's order would have robbed these people of their livelihood.

After the court battle, skirmishing continued between the two sides in every arena of public opinion. Finally a truce was achieved in 1909. The industry was ready to embrace censorship as an alternative to being put out of business. (Censorship was already established in many places, including Chicago.) A respected organization called the People's Institute of New York City was asked to form a panel to deal with movie standards. This would ultimately become the National Board of Censorship of Motion Pictures.

The movie people won public favor by showing their enthusiasm for the new board. The results were generally applauded, and many observers felt that the problem of movies and morals had been settled for good. The troubles that the industry had experienced were set down to errors accompanying its too-rapid growth, all correctable. Meanwhile the potential for good in the new medium was just beginning to be tapped. Thus to many people it appeared that the crisis was past, and all would now be smooth sailing.

When the National Board of Censorship was established, it was assumed that folks around the country would adopt the rulings of that group and save the trouble of screening movies themselves. But while this New York body did have a wide influence, it did not replace other boards throughout the nation. Even after five years there were still twenty-seven local boards in operation—much to the annoyance of certain directors. When Cecil B. DeMille submitted prints of his 1915 film *Carmen* to the various boards, each one found some part of the movie objectionable. But, complained DeMille, "No two censors objected to the same thing. They asked me to make cuts in twenty-seven different scenes!"[4]

The struggles over censorship would be repeated often in succeeding decades, but the industry had survived the first major campaign waged against it on moral grounds. Meanwhile the Great War came to occupy everyone's attention, and films entered a phase of greater seriousness. These were the years when the American movie industry was clearly coming of age, under the influence of creative masters such as D. W. Griffith, Mack Sennett, and Charlie Chaplin.

The Rise of Hollywood and a New Mythology

With the flowering of film as entertainment and even art, there came a corresponding development of the movies as "big business." Unfortunately, most of the negative elements now associated with movies also made their appearance. There was almost a buccaneering spirit among the men who rushed to capitalize on the new medium. They engaged in commercial and legal warfare over contracts, patents on new equipment, and schemes for rental and distribution.

The patent situation with movie cameras and projectors was muddled, and many of the most productive filmmakers were operating in obvious violation of the law. In such an atmosphere it became more and more desirable for some people to make their movies as far from New York as possible. Southern California was favored for its ideal weather and sunlight and also for its nearness to the Mexican border, in case legal difficulties became acute. The industry gradually centered in Hollywood, a suburb of Los Angeles which had made particularly effective efforts to lure investment.

Shortly before the First World War a change had occurred that would have a lasting impact on the industry and the nation. Up until this time moviemakers did not even name the actors in a film's credits; anonymity made it easier to keep salaries down. But a growing public demand for information could not long be denied. Finally, starting in 1910, the movie moguls decided to cash in on this public enthusiasm instead of resisting it. Almost overnight the industry found itself working on the basis of the "star system" for the promotion of its product.

The emergence of the star system coincided with the rise of the Hollywood myth. To Americans, and in fact around the world, the name "Hollywood" came to denote not so much a city as a land of dreams and a way of life separate from everyday reality. Unfortunately, it was the Mecca to which many young people traveled in search of the glittering success they envisioned there. By the 1920s Hollywood was also attracting people with the worst of motives. As more and more young people flocked to the city, all manner of establishments waited to prey on their ignorance and their ambition; unscrupulous landlords, fake talent scouts, and bogus acting studios abounded.

Against this background of corruption there emerges still another unfortunate element—the Hollywood publicity industry. The fan magazine and the sensational press quickly gained a wide audience. They found that public curiosity about the behavior of screen demigods was boundless, especially if it was *bad* behavior. Reports of immorality among the idols were irresistible to readers of the new magazines. It mattered little whether the reports were true or not—the people who inhabited this glamour world were hardly real to begin with.

If Hollywood was becoming a center of greed and indulgence, the movies it made were in keeping with the attitudes of the nation at large. Some relaxation of moral values often seems to follow a war, and in America's Jazz Age the movies were there to set the tone for fast living, freer sex, and the race for quick riches. Hollywood discovered that the postwar audience wanted to see on the screen, not ordinary people like themselves, but people who inhabited a world of comfort, wealth, and carefree elegance.

The acknowledged pioneer in depicting this type of glamour was Cecil B. DeMille. DeMille catered to public appetites with risqué films such as *Male and Female, Don't Change Your Husband,* and *Why Change Your Wife?* These films featured glamorous people in glamorous settings, and especially elegant clothing, which was often being removed. A typical ad line for one of these films was "See your favorite stars committing your favorite sins."[5]

Scandal and Reaction: The Hays Office

The postwar situation in Hollywood was too volatile to last, and it soon led to the next major crisis for movies and morality. In 1922 a series of scandals occurred that mesmerized the nation. In the worst of these, a young starlet died following an apparent rape at a movie industry party. Comedy star Roscoe "Fatty" Arbuckle, a regular in the Keystone comedies of Mack Sennett, was implicated strongly. Although court action was inconclusive (there were several trials) the incident destroyed Arbuckle's career.

This affair, along with certain revelations about other stars, was taken as proof that the worst suppositions about Hollywood life were true. The censorship debate had perked along in the background since 1920; now it seemed that a flood of public indignation might finally rise and alter the legal landscape forever. Some called for the federal government to establish control over the industry's product by way of an official government censorship office. Bills had been submitted to Congress for years with this in view, but so far none had carried.

Once again, as in 1909, leaders of the movie industry decided that some dramatic step must be taken to save them from official oversight or public disaffection. At this point, however, there were new and more powerful forces in play. Movies meant Hollywood to the public at large, because that is where they were now made. But control of the industry was in fact divided between the West Coast and New York. The studios (and the theater chains they were allied with) had turned to Wall Street to finance their phenomenal growth. Now every important step that was taken had to be in a direction approved by the bankers in the east.

In Hollywood an individual producer might be willing to flout accepted standards of decency to make a quick profit. But the conservative businessmen in their New York boardrooms took a longer view. They recognized that a public backlash spearheaded by the Catholic church, for example, could poison their investments in the new industry. Government regulation might be just as crippling. Thus they were determined to do whatever it took to fend off these threats.

To escape the dilemma, industry leaders took their cue from another big business of the day—major league baseball. In 1919 the nation had been rocked by the scandal of the Chicago "Black Sox." The baseball owners had saved their audience and their investments by setting up an independent agent to police the sport. They recruited for the task a well-known judge named Kennesaw Mountain Landis.

The major film studios agreed in 1922 to form an association called Motion Picture Producers and Distributors of America. Members pledged to abide by a common set of standards drawn up and agreed to by all. And following the lead of baseball, they recruited to head this organization a well-known public figure, Will H. Hays. Hays was postmaster general of the United States, and perhaps equally important, a respected Presbyterian elder. The plan worked, even as the baseball plan had done. The movement to establish official censorship was headed off.

For the moment, the Hays Office had saved the day for movie management. It had not done much for the quality of films, however. Many directors found formulas that were guaranteed to satisfy the stated principles of the new agreement while still working the angles of sex and vice that had been so profitable before. Mr. DeMille proved to be the master of this process—as always the first to sense a change of direction in public attitudes and the first to find a way of cashing in.

Following the establishment of the Hays Office and the new climate of moral concern, DeMille abandoned smart-set scandals and became the creator of stirring biblical epics. With *The Ten Commandments* in 1923, he found his true calling. He would focus on a biblical era for film treatment, mount a lavish production that ballyhooed authenticity, and make the crux of the film some spectacle of sin—like the revelry before the golden calf. His strategy proved successful, and he followed it through a long career.

Arthur Knight explains the DeMille legacy in these words:

Better than any other director of the era, he seems to have apprehended a basic duality in his audiences—on the one hand their tremendous eagerness to see what they considered sinful and taboo, and on the other, the fact that they could enjoy sin only if they were able to preserve their own sense of righteous respectability in the process.[6]

Other directors soon learned to adapt to the new climate of expectations. DeMille was only one of many who found ways to circumvent the reforms.

The End of the Jazz Age

The establishment of the Hays Office headed off the censorship movement of the early twenties, but debate continued through the rest of the decade. Now, however, it was over the effectiveness of the new agency. Movie critics reacted skeptically as films of the period seemed to reflect not so much a new standard of decency as a new standard of hypocrisy. Thoughtful observers who saw through the DeMille formula complained that movies actually presented almost anything in the way of immorality as long as the guilty were made to pay a horrible price in the final reel. There was a fundamental distortion of values in this approach. The "morality" of the unhappy ending was a pretense; this was not what the public was actually being enticed to see.

Concern over the Arbuckle affair and the other Hollywood scandals subsided with the passage of time. Meanwhile movie producers continued to explore every avenue of sensationalism, especially in the promotion of new stars. In contrast to the virtuous heroines of the past (in the films of D. W. Griffith, for example) new female leads such as Clara Bow and Louise Brooks displayed an aggressive sexuality, while Greta Garbo exemplified the slightly jaded woman of the world. The racy titles of the Flapper Era—*The Marriage Circle; Forbidden Fruit; Forbidden Paradise; Temptation; Parlor, Bedroom and Bath*—suggested a disregard for morality that paralleled the widespread disregard for law under Prohibition.

All the while, the Hays Office performed its function by advising filmmakers and issuing rulings on what was or was not acceptable. Hays himself was busy in what we now call public relations, creating an impression that things were going to get done, whether they actually were done or not. As the 20s wore on, the gap between promise and performance became more obvious. The MPPDA simply had not given the Hays operation enough clout. Inevitably, the old familiar complaints began to surface again.

In these unpromising circumstances an idea was born that would make a real difference. It started in 1930 with a concerned Catholic businessman, who soon gained the support of the church. He persuaded Father Daniel Lord of St. Louis University to write a detailed set of guidelines which would insure the production of wholesome, morally unobjectionable films. When the project was presented to Will Hays, he embraced it without hesitation. And so within a year, the Motion Picture Producers and Distributors of America had adopted the document as its own. The guidelines originally drawn up by Father Lord would become known universally as the Production Code, or the Hays Code.

It was several years before the MPPDA learned how to use the code. Meanwhile pressure for change continued to build. It is not surprising that the 1930s produced an upsurge of dissatisfaction and a renewal of the call for official censorship. With the onset of the Great Depression, the previous era of self-indulgence seemed sadly irrelevant.

In 1934, a bill was again introduced in the House of Representatives to provide a national censorship authority for motion pictures. In the developing national debate the single most powerful force was the Catholic church; because of its centralized authority it could marshal unified activity (such as theater boycotts) on an impressive scale. Already Catholics had formed an organization called the Legion of Decency to fight the growing immorality of movies.

A large cross-section of the public seems to have applauded the efforts of the Legion, but support among Protestant church leaders was predictably hesitant. Protestants readily acknowledged the broad common interest they shared with others in the support of public morality. However, they were not willing simply to leave it to the Catholics to establish and preserve moral standards. Here again is the basic difficulty with the concept of censorship: deciding who is to be the censor, and on what authority.

Decency's New Deal: The Production Code

Just a few years after it had supposedly gone into effect, the code adopted by Hays and the MPPDA was in danger of becoming a laughingstock.

Every producer wanted to give lip service to morality and good taste, but when it came to weighing standards against box office, there was waffling and foot-dragging everywhere. The code was administered by a small Hollywood office under Hays's authority. Rulings made by the staff could be appealed to a "jury" composed of producers representing member studios in the Association. This body proved to be hopelessly lenient, since each member of the group realized that next time around, one of *his* projects might be on trial.

Finally, when Catholic pressure was at its height and government action seemed inevitable, the movie industry took decisive action. In 1934 the Hollywood office was reorganized as the Production Code Administration. The old jury system for appeals was dropped. All appeals would have to go directly to the MPPDA board in New York. Any movie released without the seal of the Production Code would be barred from member theater chains. Furthermore, a studio releasing a film that violated the Code would get a $25,000 fine. Under its tough and dedicated administrator, Joe Breen, the Code Office would now be a power to reckon with.

The Production Code had an unprecedented impact on American filmmaking, especially in the 30s and 40s, when it was served by men of genuine commitment. The story is told in fascinating detail by Leonard Leff and Jerold Simmons in a book called *The Dame in the Kimono*. (Don't be misled by the title, taken from a line of film dialog. The tone of the book is entirely serious.) Leff and Simmons have provided a work of unusual value. Christians concerned with morality and popular culture will find in it much that is relevant today.

Under the new system things were spelled out in such detail that specific words were listed as unacceptable. The code influenced even the actors' contracts, which could now include clauses relating to moral conduct. How well it worked would depend on whom you asked, but it did unquestionably work. Its effectiveness was evidenced by the frequency of complaints against it from within the industry.

Perhaps the best known incident in the life of the Code was a ruling in regard to *Gone With the Wind* (1939) which allowed the use of Rhett Butler's famous remark, "Frankly my dear, I don't give a damn." A look into the complex negotiations that this required gives a pretty good idea of how the system worked. The word *damn* was one of those specifically forbidden by the code. But the problem here was unique given the phenomenal popularity of the novel: Everyone knew the punch line already.

There had been a huge investment of time and resources to make the movie as faithful to the book as possible. The producer argued, I think correctly, that the audience would feel betrayed if after seeing hours of faithful dramatization they were left at the end with a weaker substitute line.[7] Eventually the exception was made (by amendment to the code) and permission was granted for the use of the word. Incidentally, the final scene had been shot in two different versions—one with the "damn" and the other without—just in case.

The exception made for Rhett Butler in *Gone With the Wind* did not result in a spate of films with raw dialog, or even films about seamier characters and situations. The code maintained a vigorous life through the 40s and 50s, to the continued exasperation of directors and producers. Some of the resentment was due no doubt to missed profit opportunities, real or imagined. However, there were not a few filmmakers and critics who chafed at the restraints out of a sincere conviction that the truth was not being served the way film was capable of doing it. That is, by the accurate rendering of significant social and psychological questions, some of which related to sexual behavior.

The central influence in this period, for Hollywood and the nation, was of course World War II. Leff and Simmons provide valuable insight on how the war changed public attitudes regarding sexual morality and the role of women. Joe Breen was a staunch Catholic who believed it was the mission of the Production Code to uphold the principles of Christian morality. On the other hand, according to Leff and Simmons, "he also recognized that the war had unleashed forces that Hollywood could not ignore. The 1930 proscriptions against violence and murder, and especially adultery and illicit sex, now seemed outmoded; the endless stream of movies about fearless warriors and faithful wives old-fashioned."[8]

One of the effects of the war was to make Americans more aware of the world at large. Movies now became an important medium of exchange in the realm of ideas and attitudes. As in the years following World War I, the postwar realism of European filmmakers soon began to have repercussions here.

In drastically reduced circumstances, the movie industries of France and Italy could not hope to compete with the U.S. in mounting lavish spectacles or paying large casts of stars. For this and other reasons, leading directors in those countries were placing greater emphasis on realism than ever before. Rather than construct costly sets, for example, they might simply go into the streets to do their filming. Some of them worked untrained actors into the bargain, with surprising results. Their increased frankness in regard to sex, along with the critical acclaim they often earned, made for more headaches at the Production Code office.

The popularity of a serious film like *The Bicycle Thief* (Italy, 1950) put severe pressure on the code. When the Breen staff denied it a seal (for a brief, non-erotic scene in a brothel) a number of theater chains that were members of the association decided to show it anyway. This was the first time the membership pledge had been broken.

Of course not all European directors were serious artists like *Bicycle Thief*'s Vittorio De Sica. In the later 50s the daring exploitation of European actresses like Brigitte Bardot began to push the American industry to answer in kind. If Americans had not formed lines to see Brigitte, there would have been little interest in duplicating the type of film she appeared in. Hollywood's response centered chiefly in the female sex object whose erotic appeal was rendered harmless, as it were, by her vacuity and childishness. The prime example was Marilyn Monroe.

While Monroe, Bardot, and Gina Lollobrigida were getting the headlines and the flashy spreads in *Life* magazine, a more important story was developing in the background. The economic configuration of the movie industry was shifting in a way that would directly affect the status of the Production Code. Back in 1948, The U.S. Supreme Court had issued a ruling of far-reaching impact in the case of *U.S. v. Paramount.* In effect the court had directed the major studios to sell off the theater chains that had given them a "vertical monopoly" in entertainment. No longer could a studio control its product from the purchase of a script to the sale of tickets at the box office.

The divestiture of theater holdings took years to complete, and so it was only in the 1950s that its implications became apparent. The court had struck a blow for free enterprise, but it had also undermined the foundation of the Production Code. Compliance with the code had always depended on the discipline of studios dictating from Hollywood what films would be shown in the major theater chains around the country. After *U.S. v. Paramount*, the theaters could choose for themselves what would likely earn the most profit.

Still another factor in the changing environment was television. There were times in the 50s when the movie industry seemed on the verge of panic, believing it would lose its audience to TV. One school of thought appearing about the time of the Bardot invasion held that movies could only survive by surrendering the family trade to television and gearing themselves to more "mature" material. Fortunately, the period of anxiety was cut short as movie studios found ways of developing the new medium for their own purposes. Perhaps the biggest loser at the time was television programming, which became increasingly "harmless" and bland.

As America advanced into the 60s, there were trends almost everywhere in our culture that seemed revolutionary. Of these the so-called "sexual revolution" has had the most profound influence. It is still going on, in fact, and every new survey of contemporary habits (especially among teenagers) gives us cause to wonder about the ultimate consequences. Not surprisingly, the new attitudes toward sex that won acceptance in the 60s had a major impact on entertainment media.

In Hollywood, the Production Code Administration faced an increasingly frustrating dilemma. New and daring works by serious filmmakers made it impossible to please everybody with a ruling. In 1965 Sidney Lumet's grim, earnest *The Pawnbroker* was granted a seal although it included (for the first time in a major American film) a glimpse of female nudity. This decision pleased the more sophisticated audience but not the Legion of Decency, which refused to approve the film.

The staff at the Code Office could only look ahead with apprehension, knowing that the next controversial film might not come from a respected director like Lumet. Moreover, the traditional support that the code had enjoyed was becoming fragmented and unpredictable. The Legion itself included a growing liberal element and was often divided over what was acceptable. Prominent spokesmen from the major Protestant denominations were taking stands in favor of greater honesty and realism in films. The old rockbed constituency that Joe Breen had once enjoyed was gone.

Under the stresses of this revolutionary age, the Production Code would finally reach the end of its life. Yet the period did not bring an abandonment of the struggle over moral standards. Censorship battles continued in different parts of the country. There were new calls for government control of a medium that seemed to have lost all concern for decency.

The Response of the Sixties

The Motion Picture Association of America, as it now called itself, once again took the initiative to avoid catastrophe and maintain self-control. In 1966 the board recruited another high-profile personality to head its operations. Jack Valenti was plucked from the Johnson administration much as Will Hays had been recruited from Washington in the 20s. Valenti was to steer the agency through the next major change, and into the 90s. His practical leadership began inauspiciously. One of his first actions was to replace the original Production Code—the one that had been in place since the early 30s—with a new version. In the existing atmosphere few people took the new one seriously. To the public at large, it looked as if the industry had reached an "anything goes" condition.

In fact, the association was approaching a major turning point. While the fallout from *U.S. v. Paramount* was resulting in greater freedom for theater owners, many communities across the land were taking steps to fill the void they perceived in the enforcement of standards. Local governments were again setting up mechanisms of censorship. The old nightmare of the producers once more threatened to become reality. But this did not happen. Ironically, the furor in 1966 over *Who's Afraid of Virginia Woolf?* caused the association to identify the only viable role it could assume in the future.

After much tension and travail, *Virginia Woolf* had been granted an exemption from the code with the condition that it be publicized as a film for mature audiences only. To many observers this demonstrated the logic of a system of classification, as opposed to a simple thumbs-up or thumbs-down approach. The Supreme Court added a push in this direction when it issued two 1968 decisions relating to entertainment and decency. The decisions had a dual impact. First, it was now much more difficult to define what was or was not obscene. (Blanket censorship for the public at large thus became a thing of the past.) On the other hand, the court gave its support to the principle that communities could protect minors from exposure to unsuitable material. On this basis it appeared that the

Motion Picture Association would be able to restrict admission on an age basis without risking court interference.

In 1968 the association at last decided to do away with its code entirely and take up the classification approach. The new plan provided a rating system to specify and accommodate different audiences. This allowed a flexibility that had been impossible under the Hays Code. There were originally four rating categories: G, for general audiences; M, for mature audiences; R, for films to which no one under 16 was admitted without a parent; and X, with no one under 16 admitted, period.

The system has been modified more than once in the intervening years. The symbol PG now indicates films for which parental guidance is recommended, and the PG-13 category has been added to provide an intermediate area between PG and R. In a somewhat questionable cosmetic switch, the X was retired in 1990 and replaced by the designation NC-17. The argument was that the X symbol had been captured and exploited endlessly by pornographers. The stigma that "X" thus acquired had destroyed any market for the rare adult film that utilized strong sexual content for serious dramatic purposes.

Since 1968 the system has rated thousands of films. A few decisions are appealed each year, and about one third of the appeals result in the change of a film's designation. The system has always been an easy target for criticism, which has come from both sides of the fence—that is, those who leave a movie muttering about why it wasn't rated more severely, and those who preach that the system violates artistic freedom. Despite all the complaints, the plan has served a useful purpose in giving general guidance to audiences. It is certainly better than no help at all.

The rating system has survived by evolving gradually in response to changing public attitudes. The association carefully monitors the nation's perception of its work, and a sizeable majority still find the ratings useful. As Jack Valenti explains, "The system is like the Constitution; it has enough ambiguity built in so that it can exist in a changing world without crashing."[9]

Where We Are Now
No doubt many Christians remain dissatisfied with the kind of ambiguity Mr. Valenti refers to. However, we must bear in mind that the MPAA is a private body based in commercial enterprise. Its ultimate authority is

public opinion—precisely as the Christian's ultimate authority is not. It would hardly make sense for us to ask of a secular agency the safekeeping of values we can only derive from God's Word and the nurture of Christian teaching.

All of us must feel at times that we are witnessing a downward spiral in values, that immorality reigns in the movie industry. This is the message that Michael Medved presents in *Hollywood vs. America: Popular Culture and the War on Traditional Values*. But in spite of Medved's impressive evidence, we cannot afford to put all the blame on Hollywood. The movie industry would not last for a week if nobody bought what it was selling. The demand for G-rated films is undoubtedly stronger than many film executives realize. This doesn't change the fact that movies like *Basic Instinct* and *Indecent Proposal* go straight to the top in box-office rankings.

Before we pass judgment we should remember a few things that are less obvious than the screen sins we abhor. First there is the great question of whether movies promote immorality or simply reflect the way society has gone through the working of other forces. If the answer is some of both, as is most likely, this does not point to any radical cure for the movies. Second, we ought to think soberly of the alternatives to our current system—the possibilities of state control, or indeed church control. At what price are we willing to have our standards of righteousness enforced?

Finally, we need to guard against the generalization that all films are alike, good *or* bad, and that all moviemakers share the same values. Movie directors are as diverse in character and outlook as persons in any other field. Their work reflects it unmistakably.

I am inclined to think that today's rating code is as good as we are likely to get. Those who administer it work hard to keep abreast of public attitudes. The lessons of the past are too obvious to be ignored, and one of them is that the profits are only secure when the customers have confidence in the product. What we are left with, then, is a system that is carefully attuned to the developing *public* morality—to what most Americans feel is appropriate in terms of behavior depicted on the screen. If there is confusion in this regard among most people, then we might as well expect ratings to reflect the confusion. The system is roughly suited to the democratic civil organization we live under.

So what should we as Christians do? Should we just relax and try not to be alarmed about shifting standards? Do we cross our fingers and hope for somebody to clamp down on Hollywood with more effective censorship? Or should we just quit going to the movies and spare ourselves the grief?

Whether we like it or not, these are legitimate questions. In the next chapter I shall try to present some helpful answers.

Notes to Chapter 4

1. "Say Picture Shows Corrupt Children," *New York Times*, 24 December 1908, 4.

2. Barton W. Currie, "The Nickel Madness," *Harper's Weekly* 51 (24 August 1907): 1246.

3. "Picture Shows All Put Out Of Business," *New York Times*, 25 December 1908, 1.

4. Phil A. Koury, *Yes, Mr. DeMille* (New York: G. P. Putnam's Sons, 1959), 282.

5. Arthur Knight, *The Liveliest Art*, revised ed. (New York: New American Library, 1979), 116.

6. Knight, 117.

7. See the letter of October 20, 1939 from David O. Selznick to Will W. Hays in *Memo from David O. Selznick*, ed. Rudy Behlmer (New York: Viking Press, 1972), 229–231. Several other items of correspondence on this matter are included in the book.

8. Leonard J. Leff and Jerold L. Simmons, *The Dame in the Kimono: Hollywood, Censorship and the Production Code from the 1920s to the 1960s* (New York: Grove Weidenfeld, 1990), 126.

9. Charles Champlin, "Father of G, PG, R and X Rates 20 Years of Ratings," *Philadelphia Inquirer*, 20 November 1988, sec. H, p. 8.

Chapter 5

Taking the
Reins

I have given them your word and the world has hated them, for they are not of the world any more than I am of the world. My prayer is not that you take them out of the world but that you protect them from the evil one.
John 17:14-15

That brief historical reconnaissance in chapter 4 leaves a basic question unanswered: How do Christians respond to the screen marketplace today? (Note that the question is not about the movies, but about us.) One answer is to make the present ratings code our primary authority, and let it direct our choices. Frankly, I believe this will only lead to continuing frustration. On the other hand, if we are dissatisfied with the present system, should we yearn for a new one that would reflect our standards exactly? I am afraid this too would be a mistake.

It is tempting to consider a disinterested authority that would carry the burden for us, like a federal agency. Many Christians have inherited from our Puritan forebears an impulse to perfect America by means of government. However, I believe we must balance this impulse with a realistic awareness of where we stand in relation to our society. America in the late twentieth century is a long, long way from the Massachusetts Bay Colony.

I am reminded of Paul's outburst to the Corinthians when he learned that some were taking their disputes to secular authorities for judgment. What is striking is Paul's insistence that Christians are to be responsible for themselves—not dependent on the judgment of others. He seems almost incredulous when he asks who would dare go before the authorities with a disagreement. "Do you not know that we will judge angels? How much more the things of this life!" (1 Corinthians 6:3). Paul's exhortation to independence surely encourages us not to look to "official" authorities for guidance.

Movie Teetotalers and the Principle of Separatism

How do we proceed if official guidelines are not the answer? There are some who would urge us to go in the opposite direction. Rather than fret under codes and ratings, and mumble about the sorry state of Hollywood, they would eliminate the problem by renouncing commercial movies altogether. It is not a new idea; many adult Christians were reared in the general belief that movies were sinful, and that a Christian would sin by attending a movie. There are Christians today who adhere to this same teaching. A number of Bible colleges, for example, ask of enrolling students a pledge not to attend commercial movies.

The practice of renunciation is derived from the biblical theme of separatism, and as such it is not to be scoffed at no matter how much one may disagree with it. Many Christians of today would consider it a mistaken doctrine, while those outside the church no doubt consider it absurd. But the convinced separatists stand firm, holding to several Scripture passages for justification. The text most often cited is probably 2 Corinthians 6, where Paul urges believers not to be "yoked together" with unbelievers. He sums it up in verse 17: "Therefore come out from them and be separate, says the Lord. Touch no unclean thing and I will receive you." Paul is of course echoing a familiar Old Testament injunction: the children of Israel were to have nothing to do with customs of their neighbors, and particularly their idol cults.

The importance of this message of separation for the Old Testament Israelites is clear. It was essential, most especially, for the Jews in captivity to other peoples (see the Book of Ezra, chapter 10). In a similar way, the Christians in the early years of the church were like hostages in the culture of their own nations. The pressures to compromise, soft-pedal, and become reabsorbed into the mainstream must have been enormous for a Christian in Greece or Asia Minor. With good reason the writers of the

Epistles are so urgent in reminding new believers to hold fast to their gospel, to avoid even the appearance of compromise.

Christians today, and especially American Christians, still need to hear the message of separateness. The pressures to conform and be homogenized in the mainstream of secular culture are as great as they were in the first century, but more diverse and subtle. There is a special challenge, however, in recognizing that it is our hearts and our minds that must be separate. The external elements of life—where we go, what we do—will necessarily reflect this. On the other hand, if we are always preoccupied with external practices we risk getting the cart before the horse. We may need to jog our memories about why Jesus was forever coming into conflict with experts on external religion.

The problem now is to understand how we can be faithful to the call for separateness in a society so different from that of imperial Rome. Our society in fact originated under the leadership of Protestant Christians, many of them refugees. The forms of our culture—our political, educational, and even recreational institutions—were in many cases set up by Christian leaders. God has blessed us with this free society, and it may be that our real challenge is to be as thoroughly *in* it as we can be.

The verses quoted at the beginning of this chapter are from a passage in John's Gospel that has immeasurable significance. It is at this point that Jesus' earthly ministry was ending and the Christian church was about to be born. Chapter 17 records the prayer with which Jesus marks this momentous transition. He makes it clear that the disciples are not to be taken out of the world, but are to remain in it, sanctified and protected from evil (verses 15-17). Furthermore, he adds, "As you sent me into the world, I have sent them into the world" (verse 18). In later verses Jesus extends these provisions to all of us who have believed in him through hearing the Gospel message.

These New Testament passages indicate clearly that we are to be *in* the world. Jesus was a known *participator* in the life of this world, to the extent that he was censured for his habits (see Luke 7:33-34). We too must be in participation with our social environment. If we have been redeemed by the sacrifice of Christ at Calvary, we cannot but be different—we will in fact be cleansed and sanctified. But our separateness will consist not in *where* we are but in *what* we are. To be an effective disciple requires a skillful exercise of discrimination in being "in the world but not of it."

Finding a Positive Approach

The Christian in America is part of a society with unprecedented material advantages. Jesus told us that he came so that we might have life "to the full" (John 10:10). Christians today, more than ever before, must hear this promise with reverence and humility. Dealing with our material abundance is a formidable spiritual challenge. But in the freedom that Christ offers, we have the opportunity to be selective and to make the entertainment that we purchase wholesome and enriching.

We can learn, by God's grace, to recognize what is harmful or vacuous and pass it by, while others fall under its stupefying spell. Better still, we get to rejoice in the fine things God makes available to us even in the world of entertainment. So when a wonderful account of Christian faithfulness comes to my local theater—a film like *Chariots of Fire* or *A Man for All Seasons*—no one can deny me the right to celebrate it, or to hope for more of the same.

Even when the subject is not specifically religious, movies can offer well-made studies of moral problems that a Christian should not miss. In addition there are plenty of highly therapeutic, fun films that believers have a right to enjoy. If we feel that Christians should receive the advantages of film entertainment and film art, the problem becomes a matter of selection—weeding out that which is unworthy of our attention and seizing upon the excellent and the rewarding. The task that falls to us then is one of evaluation and the exercise of discernment.

Here is the central issue we have to deal with in these pages: Our culture presents us with the endless challenge of making choices in what we experience. In the nature of this media culture the challenge is often hidden—we don't *realize* we are being offered a choice; we aren't *aware* that we have made a decision. Nevertheless it is happening moment by moment, whenever we sit willingly in front of a lighted screen.

The crucial element for the Christian is to *be aware*. We can accept the responsibility of making our choices, steering a course that is guided firmly by our Christian values. We can also duck the responsibility. We can let go the rudder and drift in the sea of fad, sensation, and box-office "success" that is secular entertainment.

Being Pushy or Being Picky

The present rating system for movies has many weaknesses, but it is probably as much help as we are going to get from the industry itself. The complaints and quarrels will continue, and we will probably continue to be frustrated at the inaccuracy of the rating of this or that film. Perhaps it will be just as well for us to acknowledge the realities underlying the ratings, and indeed the whole concept of self-regulation in Hollywood.

The movie industry exists to make money. The powers-that-be in movies are powers because they know how to do this. Historically they show as much regard for any other values (besides profits) as they are made to by outside pressure. Their ultimate guide is the dollar, and when ticket sales start piling up in contradiction to a given set of rules, like the Hayes Code, the rules are going to change.

We need not work up a lot of self-righteous anger about this. Most Christians in America are also stout defenders of our free enterprise system; we may well think twice before denouncing those who so eagerly pursue the system's goal. After all, it isn't just in Hollywood that hypocrisy and self-interest pay off.

For example, we often hear that a movie with a PG rating will earn more than one with a G, just because of the rating. Is it the filmmaker's fault if citizens are attracted to a product that promises more sex or profanity than less? And if not, is it surprising that filmmakers will spice up a film with a little irrelevant profanity to get the more profitable rating?

That is not to say we should fold our hands. I find it particularly disgusting that movies designed for young audiences are doctored for ratings this way. But remembering that we live in a free society, I pause before going to the next step of trying to force people to make films as I would have them made. The moviemaker can reply to my complaint that if I can find something better I should buy it. Or if I can make a better film I should make it. In our free society that is the right answer.

Sadly enough, the profitability of material that is titillating or sexy has been apparent through all the cycles of the movie censorship debate. The *Literary Digest* put it succinctly back in 1924 when it stated that "the public can have clean movies when it wants them well enough to make them pay." Even then there was disheartening evidence that "many pictures worth while from a moral point of view are not worth while from the point of view of the box-office."[1]

Too often we seem to focus on the converse of this principle: not how to make good entertainment pay, but how to penalize the bad. Early in 1989 there were several news items that revealed how much impact a viewer protest could have in the area of network television. In one case a Michigan housewife gained nationwide attention with her complaint about the comedy series "Married . . . With Children." She simply wrote to the headquarters of the sponsors and told them why she objected to the show's relentless emphasis on sex. In passing she mentioned the possibility of consumer reaction against these sponsors' products if they continued to back such unwholesome material. Amazingly, her protests got results. The companies quit buying ads on that series. This took place at about the same time Pepsi-Cola was forced to withdraw a controversial spot featuring pop singer Madonna.

These developments were hailed by Christians across the land who were concerned for decency in public broadcasting. But they were not greeted with enthusiasm by everybody, and it is unclear where the majority of the public actually stood. For this reason our jubilation in such victories must be tempered with a little caution.

In the weeks following those events just referred to, there was much public debate over the sponsors' acquiescence. I was struck by a letter to my local newspaper, in which the writer plaintively asserted his right to see those things that were being curbed. Here is a portion of the letter:

> I'm not sure which bothers me more, the growing number of self-righteous, self-appointed, "protectors of American morals" who bully producers, networks and advertisers into censoring material to their own narrow-minded standards or those selfsame producers, networks and advertisers who allow a tiny, vocal minority of the population to effectively decide what the rest of us can and cannot watch.[2]

Whether we like it or not, many Americans share this writer's sentiments. They may be mistaken, but they have a perfect right to their opinion, and we Christians cannot deny them that right. The cause of the gospel is not served if people think we are out to hit them over the head with our beliefs. This is especially true when other options are available. For example, while we may admire the spunky housewife who fought back at sleaze on TV, there are those who ask why she didn't just turn the program off. (See chapter 2 on the advantages of turning off the TV!)

Let us keep in mind that there are stakes to be won and lost in any direct manipulation of the media. Unfortunately, it is easy in such matters for Christians to come across as vigilantes bent on controlling other people's freedom. We must be willing to affirm the constitutional right of free expression without shrinking from the complexities it presents today.[3]

Any action aimed at controlling media will have varied and unpredictable ramifications. Christians ought first to examine fully (as we have not done before) the ways we relate to mass media. Such an examination can be initiated by individual churches as well as larger organizations and denominations. We may find some unexplored avenues of influence that would indeed help to safeguard our values in entertainment. But our methods must be both fair and effective. A challenge so complex demands careful research, hard thinking, and hard work.*

Above all, if we are to bring forward any proposals to broadcasters or filmmakers, it must be done in a truly Christian spirit. Our aim should be to bridge the gap between us and that body of people represented by the letter-writer quoted earlier. If, for example, some coalition of Christians were to fashion a proposal to the Motion Picture Association or the TV networks, it would need to show clearly *why* we care. It should be an instrument to communicate to everyone that, rather than being killjoys, we are on the side of real happiness. Our commitment is to a Way that promotes the utmost satisfaction in personal and family life.

Any further consideration of organized pressure is beyond the scope and purpose of this book. In these pages our primary concern is with the Christian life of the individual. The options for him or her are limited when it comes to changing the way things are. The most important thing we can do is just what it has always been—to walk away from evil. Protest

---

*Popular music differs from screen entertainment in this connection (an obvious exception being MTV). Rap and other pop singers address their young audience directly; dramatic characters on the screen do not. Some of the so-called artists in pop music clearly exhort listeners to action that is immoral and illegal. This calls for a different order of corporate and legal response.

is one thing; avoidance is another. We must develop the second alternative if we wish to establish a reliable approach to commercial entertainment in our lives.

We can do much better than we have done in the past. In many Christian families the "policy" regarding entertainment is an ungainly combination of looking the other way, crossing the fingers, biting the nails, and wringing the hands—not a satisfying situation in the long run. Of course, along with it goes the regular routine of putting the blame somewhere else—on the people who make movies or on a rating system that is so unreliable. It all adds up to throwing in the towel, when we have our orders to put on God's full armor and stand fast (Ephesians 6:13).

Getting Tough . . . on Ourselves
If we are tired of feeling helpless in the status quo, then it's time we did something about it. It's time to take control. This does not mean a wave of demonstrations or a lobbying campaign in Washington. It means taking control of our own choices, and control of the boundaries of our children's options.

Let us begin with the alleged chief offender, the rating system. It can be more useful than we are making it. It will fail us if we try to make it a crutch, but by now we ought to know at least what *not* to expect from it. Those who have left the theater more than once (as I have) shaking their heads over what got by with a PG rating ought to learn. If the setting is PG we are going to have at the least some offensive language. That's the way it is if there is a *P* in front of the *G*.

There is a broad current of wishful thinking that would have the PG label to signal, "Parents, this is absolutely OK—drop Susy and Johnny off with us, and don't give another thought to what they are going to see." Such a sentiment is understandable when many of the blockbuster hits like *E.T.*—the ones kids feel they *have* to see—are in this category. But the label PG was never intended to tell parents to relax and not give it a thought. It is intended to tell parents to give some thought and use their best judgment. PG puts parents on notice that a film *does* contain elements that should be evaluated before children are allowed to attend. Many of us just aren't taking the hint.

An excellent example of the confusion and helplessness parents often feel was the case of the 1988 hit *Who Framed Roger Rabbit?* If you happened to see this movie at an afternoon matinee as I did, you no doubt stood in a long line of adults and children. I was struck by the high proportion of toddlers—not just school-age children—at the showing I attended. As the movie went by I could not help but reflect over and over on what impression these very young children were receiving.

The film was afflicted with a split personality. It had the bright colors, the cute animals, and the frenetic violence typical of cartoons, but its situations and especially its dialogue had as their primary focus . . . you guessed it, sex. In large measure the plot was generated by implied adultery. The fact that cartoon creatures were involved made it amusing for the adults in the audience. I don't know what this made it for the kids. In a way they were shortchanged, since so many of the suggestive jokes and double-entendres were not fully comprehensible to them.

Now this very fact of the "subtlety" of sex has been used to defend the showing of such fare to children. I for one am not convinced. If children are only getting half the message, they can't be better off for that. The impact of the visual code cannot be dismissed; there were not any *visual* double-entendres in *Roger Rabbit*. The sole function of the leading lady (Jessica Rabbit) was to embody sex appeal. The scene involving her nightclub act—witnessed by the "leading human," Bob Hoskins—is designed to get this across in no uncertain terms. The success of the character won "her" a salute from *Playboy* magazine.

The sexy cartoon bombshell was merely a spoof for adults—a humorous exaggeration of every screen seductress since Mae West. But this has no relevance to the needs of the child audience *Roger Rabbit* played to. The character and the context that is provided for her demonstrate one thing clearly to the *whole* audience—the idea of sex-as-commodity, or "sexiness" as something to be cultivated and exploited. The attention of all the male characters is riveted on this female type. What is the unconscious carryover for those third- or fourth-graders who experience the movie, especially the girls?

If this seems picayune, let me hasten to say that my purpose is not to condemn the movie outright. My wife and I found it highly entertaining in spots. A lot of good ideas went into the production, and a lot of fine execution. Indeed, the *idea* of spoofing the sex siren is fine. But it's not for little children. A film like *Roger Rabbit* reflects a serious confusion of values. It intends (this is made clear by its own publicity) to offer something for everyone. But there are limits to what you can throw into the pot when you want to provide wholesome family entertainment *and* titillating adult fare.

Of course the makers of *Who Framed Roger Rabbit?* must believe they can have it both ways, because the movie made them a lot of money. Furthermore, they probably believe they created a harmless, or even wholesome, entertainment for children. We cannot begrudge them their opinion. The responsibility for clarifying Christian values is not theirs; it is ours. The success of their movie is based on public confusion about values and expectations. Christian parents who unwittingly took their children to the film and came home feeling uneasy about it were simply joining in on the confusion.

Our first reaction is usually to blame the rating, when the fact is we have ourselves to blame. In a case like *Roger Rabbit* the problem is not that the PG rating is wrong, but that we *don't use it*. Parental guidance means exactly what it says. But in order to guide, parents need to have something to go on. The parent who doesn't know enough about a movie to make a wise choice should make it his or her business to find out. In a culture where entertainment is routinely based on saleability of sex and vicious-ness, we need to *know* what's in the product before we hand our children over to it.

Teamwork, and Other Untried Tactics

Now this will probably give rise to an alarming prospect: trooping down to the theater to preview every film before taking the kids back to see it. Well, that is not such a bad idea. But no parent has time to make a practice of it, even if she or he had the inclination. Fortunately, there are easier ways to learn what we need to know.

The first objective should be to give serious attention to what we read and hear about a new movie. There is a whole industry devoted to cranking out publicity; why not put it to some use serving our own purposes? With all that is written and broadcast about movies, we can usually find lots of information in advance if we simply get in the habit of looking. It is the *habit* that makes the difference. That is, checking the newspaper regularly for items about new films, turning to the movie reviews in *Time* or *Newsweek* while we wait at the doctor's office. If we don't think to investigate till the new movie has already begun playing, the magazines, TV shows, and newspaper stories about it will have passed by long since. We then have nothing better to go on in the press than the ads.

Better than relying on the press for information is reliance on someone we know who has seen the film. Here we get back to the principle of mutual assistance that was stressed in chapter 2. Within the church community we can find other parents with whom to share the duty of knowing about movies. If I am too busy this month to preview a film, perhaps I can make an agreement with another Christian parent who is free to go. An even better plan might be for parents not to depend on each other, but to seek the help of other adults with more time at their disposal. I suspect that there are retired persons in almost every church who would be delighted to share this responsibility. The cost of a ticket and even transportation to the theater would be a small price to pay in exchange for a reliable firsthand evaluation.

This practice will be most successful when the same people are involved on a regular basis. That is why churches offer us such a unique advantage. A church is a loving community where older folks can know and enjoy young families, watching kids grow up as they see them each week taking part in Sunday school, choir, etc. What a wonderful development it would be if this challenge from the media led to a way of drawing the old and isolated into useful involvement with our children and families.

None of the process needs to be formal, though it might be (a church could establish a committee to offer help to parents in just this way). It should not be conceived of as censorship or blacklisting. The information offered to parents should be just that—information. It is the parents who must decide for their children. Every family is unique, and this kind of decision should take into account the nature of the family and its members. Having more than one child, for example, presents an obvious complication: The same film may not be equally suitable for our six-year-old as for our ten-year-old. But when we do face the choice, how much better to decide on the basis of *definite* information, relayed from a dedicated fellow Christian!

In our stress on investigation and evaluation we should remember that there can be several useful results. Being prepared for what we will see, especially with our children, is often as important as the initial decision to go or not to go. For example, we may decide after careful thought that a certain film has merit and should be seen by an older child, even though it is not free of troublesome elements. The best response may be to see it with the child, not simply to run from the dilemma. We can discuss before and afterward the language or behavior presented which a Christian should not emulate. This will be possible *if* we have done our homework and can anticipate what the film involves.

The method of proxy screening and evaluation suggested here should not be concealed from the children whose interest it serves. There can be no "mystery censor" in the development of a successful policy on entertainment. So those who make use of the idea, both parents and their proxies, should be unafraid of accountability. The scout must not be shy about relating his or her honest reaction to the film in question. The parent must not be afraid of making a decision and maintaining it within the family.

There can be a decided benefit in the children's awareness of the entire process. It will establish in a child's mind the principle that we Christians interact with our culture in just the ways that we *choose* to, thoughtfully, based on our commitment to Christ. We are not simply dragged along by the tide of a popular trend or a high-intensity ad campaign.

If we can instill in our children such an attitude of Christian independence, we will have given them a gift that will appreciate in value as long as they live. This means parents being willing to say *no* and stick to it. But no one should consider saying no to a movie or show without giving a full explanation of the reasons. In fact, the giving of these reasons to a child may be the most important element. On each occasion when we do this we have an opportunity to underline our Christian values in thought and behavior. (If the occasion forces *us* to think about what our values are, so much the better.) We have a chance to teach the principle of Christian independence so often stressed in the Epistles—that is, not being "conformed to this world."

Last but not least, our patient explanation shows a child that we consider him or her *worth* an explanation. The child is not a mere vassal in a Christian family, to be taken for granted in our adult scheme of values and interests. The Christian child has to know that he or she matters as an individual, else the foundation for mature independence will be faulty. This is a point that is neglected much too often; perhaps it gets pushed aside in our continuing agitation over permissiveness. But simple respect is something children will appreciate, whether or not they agree with our decisions or even understand them fully.

The ability to make decisions and stick to them is crucial, but this is not all that is necessary. Saying no effectively—as daunting and difficult as parents find that today—is really only half of an effective policy. For many of us the greatest challenge is yet to come.

Completing the Formula

What we have stressed thus far has been the negative—things that will be decided against by the concerned parent. But if we make this our entire program, I am convinced that we will set ourselves up for failure and disappointment. We must demonstrate a capacity to recognize and affirm the good as well as to prohibit the no-good.

Our culture has many things to offer the young, and if our only interest is in singling out the bad, our children will be hard put to trust in our judgment. To avoid this we must get a head start on the matter by sharing with children our enthusiasm for the good. They must learn that the best reason to reject the sinful and the second-rate is that there is so much available that is better. It is the simple principle of using a positive example.

Taste is not developed in a void. My children will only have a good reason not to read sleazy books if they have seen me reading good books with satisfaction. They will only come to prefer excellent films over trash if I have let them sense my appreciation of a great film, if I have shared with them my understanding of the things that make it great. This obviously cannot be limited to what we see together; the point is rather that they know there are good things to be enjoyed by all of us at our appropriate levels of maturity.

Do we dare mention television in this connection? How many young people are berated by parents for what they watch, when these same parents devote hours to the smoothly packaged sex and vice TV serves up each night? As Christians we are clearly challenged to do otherwise—to do better.

The little Epistle to Titus contains some excellent pointers on what people of different ages need to be taught. Self-control is stressed repeatedly. Young women should be taught by their elders "to be self-controlled and pure, to be busy at home, to be kind" (Titus 2:5). "Similarly," we are told, "encourage the young men to be self-controlled. In everything set them an example by doing what is good. In your teaching show integrity." (Titus 2:6-7).

The forces that direct our media culture do not want us to be in control of our choices. They are more than happy to make these choices for us. But their goals are not ours, despite the millions they spend to convince us otherwise. The only way to be sure we keep heading in the right direction is to take the reins ourselves.

Notes to Chapter 5

1. "Why Vicious Movies Pay Best," *The Literary Digest* 83 (November 1924): 33.

2. William J. Levant, Letter to the Editor, *Philadelphia Inquirer*, 28 April 1989, sec. A, p. 20.

3. For a survey of current legal opinion on this issue see Patrick M. Fahey, "Advocacy Group Boycotting of Network Television Advertisers and Its Effects on Programming Content," *University of Pennsylvania Law Review* 140 (December 1991): 647–710.

PEANUTS

Chapter 6

The Language
Barrier

Brothers, stop thinking like children. In regard to evil be infants, but in your thinking be adults.
1 Corinthians 14:20

Christians who go to the movies are accustomed to coming away frustrated. Even when we enjoy them, there is often a negative footnote: *But,* we keep thinking, *they didn't need all that profanity!* I suspect that the most common complaint we have about movies these days is the language. Sexual content is easier to predict and avoid, because of frankly suggestive advertising. But dialog cannot be effectively sampled in advance. Today you never know what you will hear in a film, even it it's a dog story from Walt Disney.

The problem of foul language has received a lot of attention, and not just among Christians. In 1990 *Time* magazine featured a cover story on the blight of obscenity in movies, TV, and recordings. Spread over the garish illustration was the caption, "Dirty Words: America's Foul-Mouthed Pop Culture." As we might expect, *Time* offered a coldly objective survey that focused on a number of sociological factors. The basic findings were not new; they indicated that language habits differ in direct correspondence to economic and ethnic differences, as well as the notorious generation gap.[1]

Reading this article was a depressing experience for me, first because of the abundance of evidence, but also because, like most media analyses, it simply avoided the moral dimension of the problem. One can easily demonstrate that what is acceptable in the middle-class suburb differs from what is acceptable in the ghetto, or that most teenagers react differently than their parents do to the lyrics of rock music. But what seems to be missing these days is any perception of why one way of using language is to be preferred. Nobody is very clear on why clean is better than dirty!

The obscenity question involves complex social, legal, *and* moral factors. Christians may well be frustrated with the partial focus of media commentary. Nevertheless, we must not err on the other side by ignoring all but the abstract moral dimension (the one we are sure we understand). Abuse of language is a serious malady in our culture, but to strike at it blindly in reaction will achieve nothing. The treatment of an illness requires first a thorough examination. Let us take some time to probe the origins of our language "infection" as it is manifested in screen entertainment. Perhaps we can find some clues that offer hope for an effective remedy.

". . . and therewith curse we men"

Crude language is prevalent in movies and television for a number of reasons. Some of them relate to the dynamics of the entertainment market; others relate to the way such language fits into our daily lives. No one can deny the presence of obscenity and profanity in everyday speech, but we should be careful to observe that people use it in different ways. It can be used in a jocular and even affectionate manner. It can be used with the vehemence of rage. It can be used unconsciously, as millions of young people nowadays seem to use it. It can be used consciously to shock or offend.

Beyond these differences in purpose, there is an amazing variety in the nature and origin of the terms themselves. In the current profusion of epithets, obscenities, and swear words there is still a basic division between terms that relate to God (including, of course, his names) and those that relate to the human body and its functions. It is noteworthy that the latter are now in the ascendant.

At the middle of the century, as some of us can recall, profanity was more common in its traditional impious forms. All of the "theological" expletives, including the Lord's name and the words *damn* and *hell*, were used emphatically at moments of extreme frustration. (And they often evoked disapproval from the hearers.) Nowadays in such moments we are more likely to hear reference to functions of the body, or to its waste products. When hatred and hostility are rampant we hear the sex act invoked, after a fashion, rather than eternal punishment. The idea of damnation has less impact when so few people actually believe in hell. This shift of reference is a phenomenon that invites careful study in other settings than the present book. However, such trends may imply that what remains important is the spirit behind the word, more than the word itself.

Old-fashioned profanity or modern obscenity—styles may change, but the function does not. To evaluate the link between coarse language heard in real life and that which appears in films, we must first acknowledge a sad fact: for those who need it, *it works*. In their conscious use, those offensive words have been chosen as instruments or weapons because they do have impact. With many of them the explosiveness of the diction adds to the punch, and the satisfaction felt in their use. This is why so many obscenities begin or end with the consonant sounds known as fricatives (*f, s*, etc.) or stops (*b, p*, etc.), and are a single, abrupt syllable.

Just for a moment imagine someone in an uncontrollable rage saying "Holy body waste!" or "Copulate you!" Sounds absurd, doesn't it? But this merely testifies to the force of the words that have been replaced. The aural impact of these terms, in combination with the disgusting or taboo reference, makes them effective when the wish is to shock or injure the hearer.

This is why the words often suffice instead of angry blows. As a matter of fact, psychologists have long asserted the value of violent language as a relatively safe release valve for hostility and frustration. The same palpable force of this language is useful when the speaker is alone, just as when we indulge in a physical gesture like kicking something or pounding a table with our fist.

When we consider that expletives and obscenities are little weapons of violence, we can focus on the essential reason why Christians avoid their use. Or, it is better to say, why the mature Christian has *no use for them*. The very anger that so easily calls forth these words in the life of the world is something that should become foreign to us as we grow in the Lord. The feeling of helpless frustration when things go wrong, that prompts so much cursing, is rare to the Christian. For when we know the redeeming grace of God, we are never helpless. If we cannot believe this, our faith isn't worth much.

With this in mind, we can better understand why the writers of the New Testament so regularly link sinful words to the interior sin they represent. In Luke 6:45 Jesus says, "The good man brings good things out of the good stored up in his heart, and the evil man brings evil things out of the evil stored up in his heart. For out of the overflow of his heart his mouth speaks." Other important passages are Colossians 3:8, 1 Timothy 4:12, and James 3:9-10, where we read, "With the tongue we praise our Lord and Father, and with it we curse men. . . . My brothers, this should not be."

A Different Kind of Pollution Index
The fact of the world's sin may never have been more obvious than it is today. The ever-present crudeness of language is a fair indicator of the way many non-Christians perceive their situation. When foul language is ubiquitous in daily life, we should not be surprised that it occurs in so much of our screen entertainment. There are certain circumstances for which I believe violent and obscene words are justified in film. However, the objectionable language common in TV shows and films marketed as *pure entertainment* (and this is where the bulk of it is heard) is there for no good reason.

We hardly need statistics, but it is sobering to get exact figures such as those offered by John Leo in an essay for *U.S. News and World Report.* According to Leo's scorecard, the notorious *F*-word appeared 93 times in a single Broadway play—David Mamet's *Glengarry Glen Ross* (which received a Pulitzer Prize). A taped performance by Eddie Murphy featured the same word 214 times—unfortunately, no surprise. More to the point, and more devastating, was the case of the popular 1988 movie *Adventures in Babysitting.* Here the *F*-word is heard 13 times. As Leo points out, this is a film in which the average age of the main characters is thirteen years, and the average age of its audience probably not much higher.[2]

The reason for obscene language in a film such as *Adventures in Babysitting* is the simple, crass instinct to exploit. We are not talking about an esoteric art film; a feature such as this is commercial from start to finish. The choice of language must be based on the notion that foul language sells, especially to the teenage audience. Whether or not this is really true, industry executives *believe* it is true, and that's what they are acting on. But we must recognize that they have more to go on than mere supposition. It is not coincidence that the increase in vulgar language has accompanied a tremendous expansion of the youth market.

The shock value of "dirty" words has long made them a popular means of expressing adolescent rebellion. Movies were hardly the first medium to exploit this factor. Those who remember the beginnings of rock-and-roll, as I do, can recall pop songs from the 50s and 60s that traded on the teasing *suggestion* of a swear word when the word itself was actually omitted. Broadway could employ the same trick: What were we to make of the song in *West Side Story* that ends with "Gee, Officer Krupke . . . krup you"? The trick has now become useless since it depends on an environment where those words are in fact avoided. Nothing is avoided today.

The middle and late 60s were watershed years in the status of profanity. This was a time when everyone was obsessed with revolution; new causes were passionately advanced and old traditions passionately defended. The nation was seeing a nasty, frustrating jungle war on display in its living rooms each evening. It is hardly surprising that the graphic, obscene slang of the "dog soldiers" would be taken up by young people who identified with them, and/or who became caught up in the opposition to this war.

Crude language had long been a means of rebellion among relatively powerless individuals. It was now taken up by those who saw themselves as engaged in various forms of revolution against the Establishment. The newly popular obscenities served as weapons to offend, and as a verbal code of solidarity for the protest generation. There were confrontations in which government figures expressed outrage at the verbal obscenity of the protesters, while protesters retorted that it was more obscene to pursue policies in Vietnam that killed women and children. No one was ever convinced of the other side's arguments. No one was *listening* to the other side.

The movie world could not remain unaffected by such ferment. As we have seen earlier, the old Hays Code was finally abandoned in 1966, and movies began to appear that were in sharp contrast to those of a few years earlier. One film that was particularly notorious for its ground-breaking dialogue was *Who's Afraid of Virginia Woolf?* The movie was based on

Edward Albee's play, but there was little alteration in the color of the language when the play reached the screen. (Such a verbal cleanup had been routine with the Tennessee Williams plays of the 50s.)

Virginia Woolf centered on the tortured relationship of a professor and his wife (played by Richard Burton and Elizabeth Taylor), and the crude violence of their exchanges left nothing to the imagination. Taylor won the Academy Award as best actress for her performance. The film created predictable controversy and established a precedent in verbal boldness that few would want to go beyond. However, it was never considered anything other than a serious work for adults, and heavy going for most of them.

No-holds-barred dialogue did not sweep through the film world overnight. However, as the late 60s led into the 70s, movies on mature themes began to feature more "realistic" language, with no cushioning for the sensibilities of the audience. *Midnight Cowboy* (Best Picture Academy Award, 1969), *The French Connection* (Best Picture, 1971) and most of the features with new star Jack Nicholson, such as *The Last Detail* (1973) and *One Flew Over the Cuckoo's Nest* (Best Picture, 1975) are prominent examples.

These films were without exception serious treatments of adult themes. They all featured complex, troubled characters in grimly un-ideal settings. Anyone who didn't want to be exposed to such matter knew to stay away. By contrast, today's films present us with language that is equally coarse, even when they are made as nothing more than escapist adventure or comedy.

New Trends—Mostly Downward

Most Christians, I believe, understand the difference between pure entertainment for a general audience and realistic drama for mature viewers. They could accept the application of different standards for a comedy about babysitting on the one hand, and a tragic portrait of a working-class hero on the other. Unfortunately, in regard to language no such distinction is now being made.

Both Hollywood and a passive, uncertain public are responsible for the current problem. It's too bad that during those years of ferment just referred to, no one could point out and preserve the lines of distinction that have been lost. The entertainment media and the public might have gained a new awareness of a simple but important principle: Our popular arts should serve more purposes than one. We Christians might have stepped forward to affirm the need for honesty and artistic integrity in their proper place, while we also laid claim to a protected, wholesome sector of entertainment for children and families.

In those years of transition—the late 60s and the 70s—one trend emerged that seems especially indicative of what is wrong today. While there were stark dramas, war movies, and other films that were predictably profane, this new convention exploited crude language from a different angle. We might call it Hollywood's discovery of a "cuteness factor" in connection with bad language. It functions whenever the offensive (formerly taboo) words are given to characters who are otherwise innocent or childlike, and most typically when they are in fact children.

The earliest phase of this cute-crude phenomenon seems to have involved female characters. Up until the modern women's movement, the female half of society was not expected to use strong language, or even to understand all of it. This was regularly reflected on the screen. Movie heroines, especially the love interest, never went much beyond the "fiddle-dee-dee" of Scarlett O'Hara. There were clear indications that the wisecracking ladies played by Mae West or Jean Harlow could hold their own in a swearing match, but this was never made explicit. It did not have to be.

When the great shift began in the 60s, moviemakers (all men, of course) came to recognize the potential shock and/or comic value in having a woman utter taboo words. The trend was foreshadowed in *My Fair Lady*, which appeared on the screen in 1964. One of the film's memorable comic moments occurs when Eliza Doolittle, nervously appearing in society at the Ascot racetrack, forgets herself in the excitement of watching the race. Reverting to the language of her slum background, she yells at the horse to "move his arse." Her well-bred companions react with horrified stares, and the audience inevitably dissolves in laughter.

Of course the audience remains in complete sympathy with Eliza. Her spontaneous outburst is a satirical dart used to puncture the balloon of social pretense. The tactic was to become popular with other filmmakers, who would employ increasingly bad language. (The Broadway musical of today, incidentally, is an unfailing reservoir of profanity.) It became a cliché to use profanity as a mark of honesty or spontaneity in a sympathetic character—usually someone pitted against other characters of superior status who are made to look like hypocrites.

As the ratings code became established in the late 60s, the trend of foul-mouthed femininity gradually took shape. A prominent example is *The Owl and the Pussycat,* a popular comedy of 1970. In this feature Barbra Streisand played a free-spoken New York prostitute (an up-to-date cousin of Eliza Doolittle) who complicates the life of a priggish would-be writer living next door (George Segal).

I remember seeing the film, and enjoying many of its comic scenes. I also remember being slightly stunned when an irate Streisand let fly with the famous F-word. It was the first time I had heard it in a movie, and it may have been the first time it was actually used. Of course this one line created a lot of comment. There were some who hailed it as an important breakthrough in the struggle for greater frankness and honesty on the screen. (The movie itself was R-rated under the new system.) Some of us were *not* pleased with the "breakthrough," wondering what it might portend for the future. A lot of people probably didn't know *what* to think. But the R-rated comedy was here to stay.

It was predictable that the next phase of cute profanity would involve children. The landmark in this development was probably *The Bad News Bears,* a highly successful comedy about little league baseball players which appeared in 1976. Of course the linking of children and profanity was not unheard of even then. Many children go through a phase of showing off tabu words just to get attention. Besides this, many families have a favorite tale to tell of a child using such a word with complete incomprehension of its meaning.

This type of real human behavior was treated with warm insight and honesty in the 1962 film *To Kill a Mockingbird.* In a dinner-table scene, the father (played by Gregory Peck) patiently and firmly corrects his little girl when she asks someone to "pass the damn ham." In this scene—drawn carefully from the novel—we see a child behaving childishly. We are invited to smile, but we never for a moment lose touch with the story's basic subtext, which involves the loving transfer of values from parent to child.

When we compare what happens in *To Kill a Mockingbird* with the freewheeling script of *The Bad News Bears,* there is a sad contrast. In the latter case, which is now more or less the norm, profanity seems to be laid on for its own sake. The adult-child relationship is about as far from *To Kill a Mockingbird* as it could be. In fairness we should note that much of *Bad News Bears* was well done, that the performances were excellent. But the use of profanity here is a perfect illustration of what the term *gratuitous* means. If we need any at all, we don't need this much.

Since the 70s the use of foul-mouthed children has become a standard, tired convention in films. A major example is the mega-hit *E.T.—the Extra-Terrestrial*. In many ways this film is a masterpiece, deserving of its great success. Yet here again, years after it could be considered fresh or innovative, we see offensive language given to little children with no compelling purpose. But audiences laugh. One suspects that now they laugh just because they think they're supposed to laugh. It is a convention that we seem to be stuck with for a long time to come.

E.T.'s director, Steven Spielberg, the acknowledged wizard of entertainment for children, may have achieved the ultimate in verbal exploitation with *Indiana Jones and the Last Crusade*. This highly successful film was enjoyable for its action sequences and the by-play between Sean Connery and Harrison Ford as father and son. On the other hand it presented audiences with horrendous distortions of Christian doctrine, especially in regard to eternal life.

With respect to the language question, there is an interesting moment where the action pauses in mid-chase as father and son are pursued by Nazis. The younger Indiana blurts out the name of Christ as an oath. His father slaps him in the face, saying it is for his blasphemy. Now one must admit that in today's environment this is an extremely unusual exchange. Some members of the audience no doubt take it as an affirmation of piety. (Perhaps they forget that this same father and son are quarreling over the fact that they have recently slept with the same woman.) But while old-fashioned values are thus superficially maintained, the rest of the audience is still being offered a profane modern hero. The director is having it both ways. This is hardly an indication of real regard for the One whose name has been exploited.

Different Goals, Different Guidelines

We have been discussing unwarranted uses of offensive language in films. The films mentioned are of various types where such language is unnecessary—movies that appeal to children and young people, in particular. Most Christians will join or support any reasonable efforts to discourage this practice. The simplest and best tactic is a refusal to spend money on the offending films.

But there are other types of movies where different expectations will apply. Here the restraint that is desirable in the films we have been discussing would be inappropriate. For this second category it is necessary to accept, in the context of the drama, words and expressions that are alien and even abhorrent to conscientious believers.

I am aware that this may not be a popular suggestion with many Christians. One offers it with some reluctance; the wise writer will try to avoid saying anything that may put off a major portion of his readers. But my hope is that those who view things differently will be patient a little while, so that another side of the problem may be seen and considered. As I stated earlier, it is not important that people agree with everything set forth here. The important thing is that by serious, honest consideration each of us can come to know with greater clarity what he or she thinks, and why. This will make us better able to harmonize our entertainment choices with productive Christian living.

Why is the "language barrier" a source of disagreement among Christians? Why are there such frequent arguments, for example, between Christian parents and their teenage children over whether or not a movie is fit to be seen? There are several reasons for this troublesome phenomenon. Two in particular stand out in my own observation. The first, one that typically divides generations, is merely the factor of what we are accustomed to. Parents who grew up in a period so different from today naturally find it hard to tolerate the new lack of restraints. Their children, on the other hand, have entered a world where profanity is commonplace: in the schoolroom, on the playing field, on bumper stickers and T-shirts— everywhere except at home and at church. It is unfortunate, but hardly surprising, that young people are unfazed by bad language on the screen.

That vast difference between the worlds we grew up in makes for a nagging disharmony in the way we judge entertainment. Neither parents nor children are to be blamed for the situation. It is one that needs to be acknowledged and understood before we can make progress toward reconciliation. Churches ought to address such a problem continually in classes, study groups, and retreats, in order to help parents and children to interact and grow together. We can do better than a status quo of kids rolling their eyes at parental complaints, and parents wishing for the good old days.

The second source of disagreement regarding the language barrier is one that can be manifest between persons of any age. It is easier to identify than to explain. On the surface it appears simple: people have a different fundamental concept of what a movie is supposed to be. A great many people see the movies as a source of entertainment, nothing more. Other people, while not denying the pleasures of entertainment, would also claim for films the function of communicating ideas, or of producing an experience significant for reasons other than pleasure or excitement.

While this basic difference in attitude offers scope for a much broader analysis, let us concentrate for the moment on how the two points of view relate to language. The person who only watches movies for simple enjoyment or diversion, if he or she is a strong Christian, will be dismayed repeatedly by the intrusion of bad language. The comedy that otherwise would have been so much fun is irreparably marred. The action-packed adventure featuring a favorite childhood hero disappoints us because of the profanity. (There may be a dimension of violence or sexual activity which is just as disappointing, but our focus for the moment remains on language.)

For those whose movie interests are limited to the mainstream of romance and escapism, the product has become hopelessly tainted. People in this category are likely to be heard saying, "I wish they would make movies the way they used to . . . the way they did when I was young." Back then, they will tell you, movies were filled with excitement and breast-heaving passion, but they were still "clean"—one didn't hear actual obscenities, for example. For those who hold to this viewpoint the VCR can be an incalculable boon. Many of the great films from our childhood years, and/or from Hollywood's golden age, can now be seen again. Moreover, for those with cable television, certain channels such as AMC feature classic films almost exclusively.

For people who see in films more possibilities than simple diversion, the impact of the language problem must necessarily be different. The expectation of serious content in a movie calls for a different framework of judgment within which the moviemaker is allowed to work. To start with, a greater premium is placed on faithfulness to reality than we find in escapist fare.

With the "good-clean-entertainment" school there is an unstated agreement between creator and audience that the depiction of life will be idealized or at least simplified. This relationship between filmmaker and audience requires stories with a happy ending, or else a *satisfying* ending, where the good characters win out and evil is appropriately punished. But with more serious films the reverse is true in the way audience and creator relate. Here we expect what we see to be true to life in all its complexity, and the conscientious filmmaker will use all of his skill and resources to capture the truth as fully as possible.

And there's the rub when it comes to language. If a film is going to treat the lives of real people, it has to present them in the way they really speak and act, or it will fail. As an image of reality it will be false. This is the case in today's world, whether you are talking about soldiers in combat, members of a baseball team, or the men *and women* in a corporate board room.

Unpleasant as it is, profanity may be needed in a film for several reasons. The requirement may be to create a lifelike setting if the story involves police work, commercial sports, or ghetto life. A "cleaned-up" script for dozens of settings such as this would become as artificial as plastic flowers on a winter lawn. There are those who would object that it was not always so, pointing to well-known gangster films or war movies from the fifties that were done without the popular obscenities of today. But this objection is putting the problem backwards. The reason a lifelike film can't be made that way today is, precisely, that today things are not the way they were then.

All Christians should regret the transition from an age of innocence and gentleness to one of brutality and corruption (we need not pause to question just how innocent any other period was). However, to be always in mourning for the past and to stop our ears against the speech of our neighbors today is to hide from our lot as disciples.

Maybe we should go back and reread the story of Jonah. It is one of my all-time favorites, for the simple reason that this man was so much like me. Jonah got into trouble when he decided to disobey the Lord's command to go to Nineveh. He headed the other way instead—for Joppa and a bigger problem than he ever imagined!

What we have to remember about Jonah is that he had some excellent reasons for wanting to avoid Nineveh. After all, there were some pretty rough characters over there. (They weren't brought up the way he was.) It looked to be a thoroughly unpleasant experience. This kind of reasoning would have made sense to me, anyway. But it wasn't God's reasoning.

God knew better than anyone else how bad they were in Ninevah. But he used the lesson of the sheltering vine to reveal to Jonah something about his compassion. There is a rare poignance in the declaration at the end of the book: "You have been concerned about this vine, though you did not tend it or make it grow. . . . But Ninevah has more than a hundred and twenty thousand people who cannot tell their right hand from their left. . . . Should I not be concerned about that great city?" (Jonah 4:10-11). Jonah was concerned about his comfort; God was concerned for a sinful population in their helplessness. To make a difference, Jonah had to be there among them.

Let us not make the mistake of pigeon-holing Jonah's story as a lesson that relates only to missionaries. What we must not overlook is that God cares for sinful persons *even though he knows them as they really are*. We ourselves must not try to hide from a sinful world out of fear for our own purity or tender sensibilities. We must not because there is a subtle seduction lying in wait for us. "If such wickedness exists, then I don't have to expose myself to it," slips easily into "Why should it matter to me—I don't know anything about it." The movies—the ones that are concerned to tell the truth—can help us to deal with this temptation. But we have to be willing to let them.

A Shortage of Angels

We have discussed the validity of bad language in recreating a setting. It is probably more important nowadays in recreating an individual character. There can only be so many films about Sir Thomas More or Corrie ten Boom. The human subjects that have inspired memorable film treatments in recent years have often been flawed characters, individuals driven to extremity by circumstances or their own errant judgment. Think of the soldiers in all of the Vietnam epics from *The Deer Hunter* to *Casualties of War*; the members of torn families in *Kramer vs. Kramer, On Golden Pond, The Color Purple*, or *Rain Man*; the memorable outcasts at bay in *One Flew Over the Cuckoo's Nest, Taxi Driver*, or *My Left Foot*.

Such films have given to the American public unforgettable characters. By entering briefly into their lives, we have been able to open our eyes to what we would never experience ourselves. We could take part in suffering, temptation, and triumph that were often rendered with unimpeachable honesty. It would not have worked if these screen characterizations had not been as vivid as they were. And they could not have been so if they had not included the language people actually speak.

Now I can still hear the devotee of good clean entertainment saying, "Yes, we've heard all this about realism before. But I already *know* how things are in the world, so why do I need to have my nose rubbed in it when I just want to be entertained?" This is a valid argument up to a point. But sometimes those Christians who protest loudest against offensive dialog are sheltering themselves for the sake of their own emotional comfort. The reaction suggests that they cannot feel secure around people whose condition is in any way offensive—it may be unkempt clothes, unwashed bodies, or soiled speech. This fear of contamination affects us all from time to time. But the Christ who calls us to follow him kept company with an amazing variety of "low-life" persons.

I have known soldiers of all ranks who could not deal with the hardships of overseas duty without expressing themselves obscenely or making blasphemous references to a God they hardly knew. I am convinced that the Christian's responsibility is first to help such persons overcome their hardships, or better, learn to know God. After this one can worry about correcting their language.

I have known, as a teacher in public school, hundreds of persons who were unprepared to deal with the bumpy road of adolescent life without the use of obscene language. Their expressions would offend and grieve me because they seemed so unnecessary. What a poor, shabby device is an ugly word! But it does have its effect. It is useful to those who fear for their sense of importance, who are afraid of not being taken seriously.

There is something similar at work in the youngster who needs to have a cigarette hanging from his or her lip. My first reaction to this is usually contempt—what an absurd crutch for the ego! But if the cigarette *is* a crutch, then it could hardly be an expression of Christian love to snatch it away. The only way one could do this well would be to give something in return—preferably the gift of that Love which can make crutches unnecessary. Perhaps the same care is called for in our objections to offensive language.

Before we try to take away this or any other crutch of the weak and the confused—those who cannot tell the right hand from the left—we need to be reminded that we are called to love them too. This is a point at which the arts can help us, and none more readily than the movies.

It is easy to give a wide berth to the obnoxious character on the sidewalk, or to build a psychological wall to separate us from those who offend at work or at school. But a well-done movie can draw us into the experience of such a person as we would shun in daily life. It sneaks them past our defenses and arouses in us the love and compassion we ought to feel in the real world. The question is not whether we accept such people's speech and behavior. It is whether we accept such people.

Nineveh lies in all directions from our comfortable suburban homes. The world that God still loves consists in part of ghettos and drug dens and shacks, of people who sleep in cars and illegal immigrants who have not even that much shelter. It is the world Jesus chose not to avoid, but to enter. As we are reminded pointedly in Romans 5:8, "God demonstrates his own love for us in this: While we were still sinners, Christ died for us."

We are called to love our neighbors while they are still sinners. They may be weighed down with guilt and frustration or their helplessness without God. Often enough they reveal these conditions through the brutality and ugliness of the words they use. Our assigned strategy as Christians is *to love them anyway*. As we have seen, the movies can help us in this. But a movie cannot deal with such people convincingly if it doesn't speak their language.

In Thought and Word and Deed

What I have called the language barrier in screen entertainment is a problem of many dimensions. We shall not have covered them all, but one other point that must be dealt with is the question of whether or not exposure leads to imitation: Are we more likely to let an expletive slip out because we have heard it often in the movies?

The answer to this question depends on the maturity of the individual. No one is ready for the experience of adult films if he has not really grown up. Certainly one of the reasons we don't want children to hear cursing and obscenity is that children so often imitate. Whether they might adopt the kind of verbal brutality they are exposed to on the screen is an entirely legitimate concern. How they react to what they hear in daily life is no less crucial. By far the most important influence is the example set by parents and other adult models. We must protect our children from needless exposure in entertainment, but we must give them the pattern in ourselves of that faith that makes violent language irrelevant.

It must be understood that to allow ourselves to hear objectionable language in a dramatic setting is not to condone this language. From the way some Christians discuss movies, one would think that the Christian life was a matter of keeping our ears free from pollution. Nothing seems to arouse so much indignation as the unpleasant coloring of language. Why are we not just as annoyed over the depiction of sinful actions?

Many of us watch the news each evening with the dedication of addicts. Much of what we see is deplorable, and much is truly indecent. Yet instead of being ashamed to watch, we feel rather virtuous for making ourselves informed citizens. Problematic language deserves at least this much detachment. If the presence of offensive words becomes the governing criterion of our movie preference, we handicap our minds and blunt our perception of the world we are called to minister to.

I have tried in this chapter to redraw some distinctions that often get blurred in moments of alarm and indignation. I would urge Christians not to mix in apples when they are trying to make a judgment about oranges. Movies do many different things, and moviemakers are amazingly diverse in their values and intentions. It is important that we consider the full range of what films have to offer to all of us—children and adults, on our own and in our families.

Surely we must be concerned with what our children hear, and what might make a harmful impression on them. We cannot be too vigilant in weighing and selecting their entertainment experiences. (That is one of the reasons this book begins with a hard look at television.) On the other hand, we as adults should not cut ourselves off unthinkingly from the sincere and honest work of our best artists.

Here it may be helpful to remember Paul's words in 1 Corinthians 13 about growing up and replacing childhood attitudes with mature ones. Yes, it is tempting for us to cling to the charm of youthful experiences, to wish for the kind of innocent thrill that certain movies gave us as children. None of this modern complexity of motives . . . no need for sex or real, contemporary evil (or language) to intrude. But such an attitude can hardly help us to Christian adulthood.

Paul was speaking in 1 Corinthians of maturation of spiritual matters, but his reference to putting away childish things deserves a broad application. In the realm of screen entertainment there are serious artists at work whose goal is to help us see and help us care for the world as bad as it is. Their work is an undeniable resource for building Christian awareness. Would Paul reject such a resource if he were with us today?

Notes to Chapter 6

1. Richard Corliss, "X Rated," *Time*, 7 May 1990, 92–99.

2. John Leo, "Somebody Ought to Give a Darn," *U.S. News & World Report*, 7 November 1988, 78. Michael Medved presents similar statistical data in *Hollywood vs. America: Popular Culture and the War on Traditional Values* (New York: HarperCollins/Zondervan, 1992).

Chapter 7

That's
Entertainment?

For not to irksome toil, but to delight
He made us, and delight to reason joined.
John Milton, *Paradise Lost*

Have you ever been sitting in a movie audience when suddenly you were aware of a big grin on your face, and there was no telling how long it had been there? I have. It can even give me a momentary sense of embarrassment; sometimes I steal a look at the people around me to see if they are enjoying themselves as much as I am. The movie doesn't have to be a comedy—it can be a thriller, an adventure story, or a tense drama. The pleasure of being well entertained is somehow the same.

Of course movies don't always produce this effect. Sometimes the smile never comes. After paying my money and spending my time, I find I am *not* entertained. Moreover, there are some films that give me excitement or make me laugh a lot, but leave a faint aftertaste that reminds me they did not appeal to my better instincts. They may even have encouraged certain attitudes that as a Christian I should be trying to leave behind me.

The focus of this chapter will be on what entertains us, and why. This is always a popular topic of conversation. It's something we think about often but never very deeply; we know what we like, but most of us would be hard put to say why.

If you asked me to name some favorites in terms of pure entertainment, I would probably start with the films of Ginger Rogers and Fred Astaire.

I recall a time not long ago when my wife, Ruth Ellen, was under a great deal of stress at work. When the pressure was finally off (she had been handling the preparations for an office move) we knew it was important for her to relax and unwind. On the evening of D-day, when the move was successfully completed, we pulled out a video we had picked up a few days earlier at the public library. It was the 1935 classic *Top Hat*, one of Fred and Ginger's best.

We made a pot of coffee (Dutch chocolate almond—Ruthi's favorite), then sat back and propped our feet up as the old RKO broadcast tower signalled the start of the film. It couldn't have been more fun—Astaire's dancing simply defies you not to feel good, and Rogers is an amazing combination of shimmering elegance and down-to-earth spunk. (I had heard of these two legends all my life, but only came to appreciate them as an adult, courtesy of the VCR.) When Ruth Ellen and I weren't catching our breath at the dancing, we were laughing out loud at dialog that still crackles with wit. And, oh yes, there was music by a man named Irving Berlin. I can't speak for Ruth Ellen, but I went around for the next two days humming "Puttin' on the Ritz." The smile was definitely there for *Top Hat*.

In referring to this film and the pleasure it gave us, I must point out a fact that seems commonplace but is quite significant: *Top Hat* was very much like all the other Astaire/Rogers movies I've seen. This is a familiar attribute of films that succeed impressively as entertainment. There is more often than not an element of repetition or imitation.

When we think of the most successful entertainment in films, we must think in terms of groups or series: the Keystone Kops, the Thin Man, Crosby and Hope, the Pink Panther, or James Bond. Each of these names indicates not a single film but a whole series. Each one began with the discovery of a certain recipe or formula that was profitably repeatable.

The principle of the repeatable formula extends far beyond those clusters of films identified with one character or one performer (or pair). Consider the examples of the screwball comedies of the 30s, the westerns of the 40s and 50s, or the cop-buddy movies of the 80s and 90s. When there are enough of a given type, we think of them together as constituting a genre.

This phenomenon is worth looking at in some detail. There has never been a movie series more successful, for more years running, than the James Bond films. They practically qualify as a genre unto themselves.

Each of these films represents a modification of a very basic formula whose elements include (1) the patented witty but dangerous hero, (2) a quantity of sexy and available women—some on the hero's side and some on the side of the enemy, (3) an outrageous, fanciful villain or villains, and (4) eye-boggling technical gadgetry. The list could go on, but these items make the point.

The audience for James Bond came with definite expectations and enjoyed seeing these expectations fulfilled. When it comes to pure entertainment, we like the known, and the movie industry likes to give it to us. Any evaluation of the movies as entertainment (in contrast, say, to movies as an art form) cannot fail to acknowledge this. The successful formula rules unchallenged in the world of production and creative development.

The existence of formulas is neither good nor bad in itself. A talented director and cast can approach a well-worn idea and make something wonderful with it. Moreover, the presence of stable genres has helped audiences to accept and identify characters, to recognize situations and relationships for decades. On the other hand, the influence of the formula has led to untold numbers of mediocre films.

More serious from the Christian viewpoint is the fact that formulas have occasionally been developed that appeal to our worst instincts, that achieve their effects of stimulation, excitement, or amusement at the direct expense of Christian values. In the course of this chapter we will take time to examine some of these formulas and the way they function.

Principal Ingredients

Of course there is more to consider in regard to entertainment than genres or formulas. Good entertainment is a category that covers an amazing multiplicity of styles, subjects, and examples. For any one movie there may be a dozen identifiable factors that make it successful *and good*. From a technical standpoint the building blocks are obvious: plot, dialogue, casting, cinematography, and so on. When one of these is flawed or weak, the public and/or the critics react predictably and the movie's stock falls. On the other hand, one of these elements can sometimes be so superior to the usual standard that it lifts the entire film, in spite of the mediocrity of other aspects.

Strong performances by great screen personalities have overcome many an undistinguished script to make a film succeed. *Red Dust, Dark Victory, The African Queen, The Verdict,* and *Rain Man* are random examples. In nine out of ten productions there is no more important factor than the stars themselves. We shall devote much of our attention in this and other chapters to the impact of the screen star.

The musical score is another element that often lifts the rest of a production above mediocrity. Or it may be icing on an already impressive cake. *The Sting* and *Chariots of Fire* benefited enormously from their effective scoring. Disney features from *Snow White* to *Beauty and the Beast* would be treasured for their music if for nothing else. There is hardly a major classic among large-scale films that is without a memorable soundtrack (*Gone With the Wind, Lawrence of Arabia,* etc.). The films of Alfred Hitchcock offer textbook studies of how the music and the soundtrack can be used to enhance the overall effect of a drama.

A great film typically reveals a combination in which *all* of the important elements are superior, and all are integrated—made to support each other—by a director of superior skill and imagination. That is why there are relatively few great films. Unfortunately, what makes for excellence in a movie is not always what makes for popularity. It sometimes appears that the most popular screen entertainment is also the least intelligent, and certainly the least demanding of thought. But why should this be so?

To account for the phenomenon of film entertainment we must consider not only what goes into the film, but also what happens in us, the audience, when we respond. It is clear first of all that when we see an entertaining film we come away *feeling good.* We may leave a horror movie feeling good that we are alive, knowing that the world we return to is normal and safe. More often we come from a film feeling more relaxed than before because we have been made to laugh. Sometimes while enjoying a comedy we can physically sense a lifting of the weight of stress. The effect is doubly valuable when we are enabled to laugh at ourselves.

Self-forgetfulness, in fact, is one of the key elements of popular entertainment. And movies are better able to bring this about than any other art form. Movies reach this goal from many directions: comedy, adventure, nail-biting suspense, even horror. All of these can succeed in diverting our attention from normal preoccupations and worries. There is nothing wrong with escapist entertainment. On the contrary, I believe many of us make a serious mistake by not giving it enough importance. Instead of casual, unthinking consumption of such fare, we ought to take it seriously enough to look for excellence here as we do elsewhere.

There are some filmmakers whose only concern is to learn which buttons to push to get a predictable response. Their vision and purposes never go beyond the goal of manipulation, and on this basis they can become extremely successful. But there are other directors, writers, and performers who are not satisfied merely to play on the audience's known susceptibilities. They would rather find a new approach to our feelings, or an original way to use a conventional formula. It is from the latter that we have most to gain; it is their way of entertaining us that may teach us as well.

Entertaining films can do more than divert; they can also affirm. Many a comedy serves up a powerful moral lesson (see the masterpieces of Frank Capra, for example) and is no less entertaining for it. Some of the most successful amusement films in all categories involve an affirmation of Christian values. The tradition runs all the way from *Mr. Deeds Goes to Town* to *Driving Miss Daisy*. Action-filled westerns and war movies have been effective vehicles for the expression of deeply felt moral concerns.

Unfortunately, some of our most popular films do not reflect any values at all, much less Christian values. In recent years the so-called "action movie" genre has dominated the box office. Hits such as *The Terminator*, *Robocop*, *Lethal Weapon*, and *Die Hard* have crowded the territory first staked out by Clint Eastwood and Sylvester Stallone. This genre depends on slavish repetition of formulas. That is why we see the same titles from year to year with Roman numerals after them. Spectacular violence sells these movies, not character or plot. Traditional values make an occasional appearance, as with family man Danny Glover in the *Lethal Weapon* series. More often the good and the true are lost in a scramble for novel tension-packed confrontations.

The action movie is not alone in ignoring Christian values. Several new genres and sub-genres exploit formulas that undermine wholesome attitudes to sex. One of the most successful is based on a wildly romanticized view of the prostitute. The character often referred to as "the whore with a heart of gold" is a well-worn movie cliché. She has generously saved the day in countless features from *Gone With the Wind* to *The Sting* and *Trading Places*. But until recently the tradition involved a poignant regret for everything she had lost. The new formula offers instead the prostitute as a well-adjusted woman. She is even pictured as enviable in her freedom from stuffy convention. At worst she is a Cinderella, enduring her thankless existence until Prince Charming comes along to bring her fulfillment. We can gauge how profitable this new formula is by the example of such films as *Risky Business* and *Pretty Woman*.

Another sex genre, sometimes linked with the happy-hooker theme, celebrates the loss of virginity. It typically features a teenager involved with an older adult. This situation was not invented by Hollywood scriptwriters, but in the past two decades it has become a popular subject for exploitation. Two films of 1971—*The Last Picture Show* and *Summer of '42*—attempted to deal with the matter seriously and tastefully. But in Hollywood one man's good intentions become another man's good excuse. An idea that may be meaningful and worthwhile in its original treatment is seized upon by hacks for its sleaze potential.

By the mid-80s the sexual initiation formula was giving audiences the likes of *Little Darlings, My Tutor, Private Lessons,* and *Blame It on Rio* (in which a middle-aged character played by Michael Caine has an affair with his best friend's teenage daughter). These and other movies (including some of his own) foreshadow the moral calamity that Woody Allen has recently brought upon himself and those closest to him. Meanwhile movies that feature teens shopping for sexual experience with other teens have become too numerous to mention.

Each year there are fresh, original, and thoughtful films to compete with the routine Hollywood product. But the films based on can't-miss formulas are the ones that are heavily promoted and make the most money. When the latest action movie or "hot" romance surges to the top at the box office, it becomes an event that everybody must see (recall *Batman, Ghost,* or *Basic Instinct*). But for Christians the must-see syndrome can be a serious problem. What the world considers desirable, even obligatory, is often what we must avoid, according to clear New Testament principles.

We now face the question of whether "good entertainment" is the same for a Christian as it is for the rest of the world. The answer is yes and no. Christians ought to be able to enjoy much of what others enjoy, because in large measure we have the same needs as they do. We endure the same pressures and frustrations at our jobs, the same tensions at home, the same doubts and anxieties about ourselves. *We* need the load-lightening forgetfulness that movies can bring—the comedies, the escapist adventure films, the thrillers. However, though our emotional needs may be similar, our standards are not at all the same as those of the world at large.

As Paul states in Romans 8:5, "Those who live according to the sinful nature have their minds set on what that nature desires; but those who live in accordance with the Spirit have their minds set on what the Spirit desires." Unfortunately the things that the sinful nature desires are staples of mass entertainment.

Revenge—The Ultimate Formula

As we have already noted, formulas are a way of life for the movie industry. With as much money as it takes to mount a typical production, backers will always favor investment in something that has worked before. The western enjoyed decades of popularity while reworking one or two basic formulas repeatedly. Romantic melodramas by the hundreds have been constructed on similar plots that require separation and last-minute reunion. Films involving competition, athletic or otherwise, almost always follow the same course: Defeat and disappointment are replaced by exhilarating victory.

One of the most dominant elements in films of the 70s and 80s was the revenge formula. With this one an early outrage to the hero is the pretext or "justification" for a scintillating payback at the climax. Of course revenge is as old as civilization. It figures prominently in the Old Testament as well as in secular literature and legend from around the world. Some of its most refined and elaborate treatments appeared in the 19th century novel, especially in France. Examples include *The Count of Monte-Cristo, Cousin Bette, Great Expectations, The Scarlet Letter,* and *Moby Dick.*

The concept of revenge used to be presented in a far different moral context than what we see today. It was endlessly exploited as a plot-driving force, but was always presented with clear warning signs attached. The unspoken assumption was that revenge is a dangerous incentive, likely to harm the one who seeks it as much as the intended victim. This echoed somewhat the biblical dictum that vengeance belongs to the Lord (see Deuteronomy 32:35). Even when revenge was achieved by a romanticized hero such as the count of Monte-Cristo, it brought a taste of sadness and loss.

Most nineteenth- and early twentieth-century writers linked a cautious attitude toward personal revenge with a preference for the higher concept of poetic justice. According to this principle a wrongdoer is paid in full for his misdeeds; however, the retribution does not come at the hands of the wronged party, but by the workings of fate or other people. Poetic justice has been abundantly evident in the film tradition, in examples as diverse as *The Treasure of the Sierra Madre, Citizen Kane,* and *Hud.*

But these examples represent how things once were. Today, judging by much of our fiction and film, we live in a far different moral environment. Neither the idea of poetic justice nor the insight that vengeance belongs to God are considered when God himself is doubted or ignored. More and more we find stories in which wrong is only met with greater wrong. Revenge becomes not God's business but man's, and man goes about it with savage efficiency. The exploitation of this theme was most blatant in the 1970s, with the films of Charles Bronson and Clint Eastwood.

In the mid-1980s, Sylvester Stallone and Chuck Norris succeeded in adapting the revenge formula to apply not just to individuals but to an entire nation, with their back-to-Vietnam adventure films. There emerged a subgenre of movies that were essentially revenge fantasies feeding on the frustration and resentment left over from the Vietnam War. These films made millions, and everyone involved got to feel righteous and patriotic, but in reality the filmmakers were simply enriching themselves by exploiting the audience's feelings of bitterness.

The transformation, or corruption, of the revenge formula is easily traceable in the western genre. There are striking contrasts between westerns made as late as the 50s and those that appeared in the late 60s and 70s. We can see the effect just by comparing the heroes played by Gary Cooper and those portrayed by Clint Eastwood.

The Eastwood character, built on the salient qualities of the actor (squinty eyes, menacing whisper) was forged in a unique product of the 60s called the "spaghetti western." The phenomenon began in 1964 with *A Fistful of Dollars,* which was filmed in Italy. The traditional western, along with its appealing action and sentimentality, had clearly upheld certain values: integrity, loyalty, compassion, and a generous sense of fun. But in the spaghetti western and its American imitations, the hero was successful because he was meaner than the bad guys. Any evidence of Christian values was erased.

The traditional western hero placed his superior strength and skill at the service of the weak and innocent. This is the concept or myth celebrated in such classics as *Shane* and the relatively modern *The Magnificent Seven*. But the superior skills of the new hero were at the service of himself alone. It is the revenge formula that invariably gave this hero the pretext for violence—just as it would later do in the urban cop films like *Dirty Harry*.

Not Like They Used to Be

The evolution of the post–World War II movie hero has often been noted with alarm or distaste. There is a wide gulf between the Gary Cooper of *Beau Geste* and the Paul Newman of *Hud*, between the Clark Gable of *China Seas* and the Jack Nicholson of *Chinatown*. The differences in women's roles are less talked about but equally significant. After World War II dramatic roles like the ones Bette Davis and Joan Crawford had made famous simply disappeared. For the next three decades commercial films offered endless refinements on women as sex objects. The situation began to change again in the late 70s, and now Hollywood claims an abundance of strongly individual female stars. Still there are more good actresses than there are good roles for them.

These changes in the nature of movie heroes and heroines have been perceived by most of us, but not often fully understood. We can begin to sort out what they mean by first recognizing a change in the professional status of the actor. The star of the prewar generation was a product of the studio, which virtually owned him or her. The studio system routinely called for a trotting-out of the actor or actress in a number of inconsequential B-movies. The roles might vary widely until one came along that the public responded to with enthusiasm.

Thus by trial and error the studio would see that the performer found a particular image that would lead to stardom—the *persona* in which the public liked him best. From then on the star would simply appear in movie after movie offering the same persona in different situations, with different names. Actors who chose to challenge the system out of concern for their own artistic goals did so at great effort and great cost.

After World War II a new atmosphere prevailed. Stars finally became more independent; some of them eventually discovered the strategy of incorporating themselves. Movie projects were initiated by a few individuals, often the stars or their agents, and "packaged" with the contracting of cast, director, and production team for one movie only. Established actors could begin to shop for projects that appealed to them. A few major figures like Cary Grant could find a story they liked and buy themselves a production of it. The studio system was dead, and the new flexibility in film production helped to encourage a new attitude among performers. This in turn would lead to a change in the public perception of the stars.

Another factor in the changing post-war environment was the influence exerted by a new discipline known as The Method. This was an approach to acting promulgated by the teachers and directors at the Actors Studio in New York City. The Method was partly a result of the ascendancy in American life of psychoanalytic theory. Its teachers encouraged the performer to explore his own psyche, his own wells of emotion, in creating a character. When the performer succeeded, he or she might produce a truly memorable portrait. And it was the *actor* who was doing the creating, not just the playwright or script writer. The best work that resulted from this approach seemed to have an honesty, a reality, that could not be matched in an older style.

Many new stars of the 50s were products of The Method. Marlon Brando was the first to become a major screen personality, but he was soon followed by Montgomery Clift, James Dean, Lee Remick, Paul Newman, Joanne Woodward, and others. These performers achieved their impact by a more complex process than was needed for prewar heroes. It was not just what they were, but what they were set against that made younger audiences identify with them.

The concept of a hero at bay, helpless against overwhelming odds, signals the change in movie audiences that began in the 50s and continued with the rise of the teenage entertainment market. The new film protagonist, notably without power and influence, was now likely to *be* a teenager. The phenomenal popularity of James Dean, gained in only a handful of roles, showed that the young audience could relate to a hero who was confused, sensitive, vulnerable. It was a far cry from the stoic icons of the prewar world, like Cooper and Gable.

The new male stars typically portrayed individuals in a state of rebellion. Brando in his black leather jacket created a lasting image as a motorcycle gang leader in *The Wild One* (1953). Newman rose to stardom playing the maverick in films like *The Long Hot Summer* (1958) and *The Hustler* (1961). Not much later, Steve McQueen established his rebel persona as the incorrigible American prisoner in *The Great Escape* (1963). Whatever they were rebelling against, these heroes were almost always unsuccessful. They did not master their circumstances; they did not dominate other people.

One quality that young audiences of the 60s considered essential was honesty; heroes could fail miserably as long as they were true to themselves. Society and its institutions were seen more and more to be riddled with hypocrisy (this would be Dustin Hoffman's great discovery in *The Graduate*). By contrast the new hero had few illusions about society or himself. He knew who he was, or he was busy finding out, and needed no pretense. To a generation absorbed in the quest for identity the new individualist offered an attractive model.

The element of rough integrity, of being unpretentious and undeceived, may explain the rather sudden appearance of the Bogart cult among college students of the 60s and 70s. In his typical films, the Bogart character was placed in situations where he faced overwhelming odds. He was often in trouble with authority, and he usually showed it little regard. He saw through the hypocrisy and the evasions of others on both sides of the law and remained sure of who he was, true to himself.

Alistair Cooke once made an interesting comment on Bogart's rise to stardom. It was in the early 40s that the actor finally moved up from gangster pictures, where he had first established his "tough guy" image. And it was then that all of Europe was falling victim to gangsterism on an epic scale. As Cooke says, "Hitler was acting out scripts more brutal than anything dreamed of by Chicago's North Side or the Warner Brothers. . . ." People felt instinctively that it would take a shrewd, hard-edged hero to stand up to this new menace. In Cooke's words, "Bogart was the very tough gent required, and to his glory he was always, in the end, on our side."[1]

The idea of an audience that feels threatened by violence is significant. Surely it helps to explain the reception of Eastwood, Stallone, and the other macho enforcers who ruled the box office during the 70s and 80s. In modern America the fear of urban crime has replaced the fear of foreign dictators. But the mass audience still likes having a champion on "our side" who can be as nasty and brutal as the bad guys.

If we accepted this analogy without qualification, however, it would be a libel of Bogart's memory. The *difference* between Bogart and the modern action hero is what counts. In some of the great films that fixed his persona—*Casablanca, To Have and Have Not*—the Bogart hero goes through a significant development. He changes from being a callous egotist into a caring, unselfish, even noble champion of a cause beyond himself. When we look at a Dirty Harry or a Rambo we see little to compare with this; there is only personal vengeance motivated by personal grievance. Indeed, Bogart's great gift was to suggest an inner tenderness and warmth even in the most "hard-boiled" roles. With today's heroes of violence we get the sense of nothing inside at all.

Even in the 1990s, violence is the key element of many big-budget films: more cars blowing up, more hardware being employed to destroy human life. And this is predicated on more pulp evil, more revenge paraded as justice. But we must remember that movies keep recycling these familiar formulas of violence because audiences keep paying to see them.

Christians may well become frustrated when popular trends in entertainment exalt what is contrary to God's rule. Remorseless violence is not on the recommended list for us, any more than sexual titillation. But these are not the only categories that pose difficulties. The people who package car chases and seductions are always coming up with new ways to manipulate an unwary, willing audience.

Nothing More than Feelings

Those who prefer worthwhile, wholesome entertainment are often caught in a trap by the movie market. In their flight from the tiresome excesses of sex and violence, these people are targeted for innocuous mush. Sensationalism is replaced by sentimentality.

The major problem with commercially wholesome movies and television shows is that they are so often imitative. They resort to formulas routinely, showing as little originality as the cop movies or the teen sex comedies. Films that forgo the worldly allure of sex and violence need *more* imaginative freshness to be good. All too often they end up as bland illustrations of platitudes such as "Love conquers all" or "It's always darkest before the dawn."

In these uplifting films the hero errs grievously but sees the light in the end because of the influence of a saintly woman. Or the heroine struggles against overwhelming odds, falters, nearly gives up—then something urges her on and she gains success. In every case when the good triumphs, we get an easy emotional payoff. Identifying with a character who overcomes adversity, we feel heroic. Touched by the example of saintly goodness, we feel virtuous ourselves. Having been coaxed to feel sympathy, we come away thinking that we are deeply compassionate individuals.

There is nothing inherently wrong with the story lines suggested above. Every Christian believes that love (in the most basic sense) conquers all. The great *original* works that illustrate a truism like "Money can't buy happiness" have a timeless power. This is the nature of the beloved Bible stories—the Prodigal Son, Joseph and his brothers, Job. To read one of these stories is to be struck by the undiluted truth about human experience. Likewise certain great secular works focus upon the central moral truths with startling clarity.

But today's efforts to exploit goodness in entertainment are not original but counterfeit. In most cases they appear as trivial, sentimentalized films and TV shows. These productions get by largely because of an advantage we offer them. That is, the market for sentimental goodness in films is presold. When we go to a movie that we know is a heart-tugger we are already predisposed to have our emotions stirred, our hearts warmed. Banking on this attitude, moviemakers can and do take shortcuts to emotional payoffs. Thus it happens that we feel moved by productions that are in reality less than convincing, less than honest.

Sentimentality is by no means confined to stories about lost children or blighted romance. The numbing effect of this element is clearly demonstrated in the popular *Dances with Wolves*, voted Best Picture of 1990. This movie represents a great opportunity missed, because in many ways it was a superior production. The cinematography was justly praised (winning the Academy Award also); John Ford or David Lean would have been proud of such sweeping, majestic panoramas. The performances were good, too, especially those of the Indians.

The weakness of the movie is the script, which is riddled with wishful thinking and sanctimonious fraud. Unbelievable episodes such as the opening battle scene are merely the most obvious problem. These are matched by the manipulative use of the hero's beloved animals: the killings of the horse and the pet wolf put *Dances with Wolves*, for all its pretensions, in the same league with *Lassie Come Home*.

The film's worst inaccuracies are the important ones about white people and Indians. To achieve its emotional payoffs the writers resort to gross oversimplification. White people (aside from the protagonist) are all obnoxious swine or suicidal deviants. The Indians are all innocent, reasonable, and noble, except for those who have gone bad because of the stress brought on by the whites.

This moral stereotyping of the races serves the ends of the movie—to heighten the melodrama and feed into the revenge formula. But it cannot ultimately serve the cause of native Americans or anyone else. White audiences simply come away feeling good because they know *they* are superior to the fiends depicted in the film. The movie reduces a historical situation that is tragic in its political and moral complexity to a struggle between good guys and bad guys.

We can measure the limits of this film by comparing it with another movie based on a great historic tragedy—*Schindler's List*. The earlier film attacks its difficult subject earnestly, striving to be profound. It misses the mark because its creators lacked the commitment to make all of their characters fully human. They take the short cut of sentimentality—they make it easy for us to love the Indians and hate the white soldiers.

The makers of *Schindler's List* chose the hard road of moral complexity. The "hero" is greedy, unscrupulous, unfaithful in marriage. He is almost trapped into his change of heart. The principal "villain" is terrible indeed, yet Amon Goeth (as played brilliantly by Ralph Fiennes) is a human being. We grieve for his moral failure even while we are horrified for his victims. The movie doesn't make it easy for us to hate him, or, for that matter, the German soldiers in general.

Schindler's List grapples with evil head on; there are no ideological blinders, no emotional cushions. If its creators had chosen to go for short cuts and sentimentality, they could still have made a successful movie. They would not have created what we have now—a work of art that is truly profound.

Sentimentality in art (or in thought) is not always easy to detect. And though we take the term for granted, it is not so easy to define. The best definition I know is given by Laurence Perrine in his classic textbook on poetry, *Sound and Sense*. "Sentimentality is indulgence in emotion for its own sake," he wrote, "or expression of more emotion than an occasion warrants." His further comments are as appropriate to film as to the written word:

> Sentimental *literature* is "tear-jerking" literature. It aims primarily at stimulating the emotions directly rather than at communicating experience truly and freshly; it depends on trite and well-tried formulas for exciting emotion. . . . It oversimplifies; it is unfaithful to the full complexity of human experience.[2]

If we are to be warned against sentimentality in literature, we need to be doubly wary of it in the movies. There the chances for cheaply purchased emotional effects are magnified. What the writer must labor for with many lines, the camera can do with one close-up of a child in tears, or a long shot of lovers walking on the beach.

Movies have never been reluctant to go for all the sentiment they could manufacture, from the early silents with their helpless Victorian heroines to modern tales of male and female bonding. From *Penny Serenade* to the sugar-coated silliness of *Field of Dreams*, the list keeps on growing. Television offers examples every night. Recent TV advertising has displayed the most shameless contrivances to exploit our feelings. Love and warmth sell everything from beer to automobile tires to a hitch in the Army.

The wholesome movie that relies on sentimentality for its appeal is rarely a great one. In fact, few of this type are very good, and we should not kid ourselves about their mediocrity out of desperation. On the other hand, many people, especially if they are intellectually sophisticated, go overboard in the opposite direction and think that all sentiment is bad. This too is a mistake. If we threw out sentimentality we would have little left of Dickens or Verdi, much less Walter Scott or Stephen Foster. And of course we would have no *Casablanca* or *It's a Wonderful Life*.

I think some Christians are susceptible to the appeal of sentimentality because we are so attuned to the importance of love in our lives. Love is an essential part of our faith and our way of looking at the world. It is the overarching theme of the Bible. So how can any portrayal of love be bad?

Here is an important truth that we need to learn when we confront popular entertainment: *Love* is one of those words that can mean a hundred different things, depending on the user. People plug it into the most amazing assortment of situations regarding sexual partners, children, pets, flags, foods, even automobiles ("I love what you do for me"). The real thing cuts much deeper than most of these popular uses would suggest. It has as much to do with pain and sacrifice as with warm stirrings of the emotions. Christians must be cautious about sentimentality for the very reason that we are serious about *love*.

There is a brief scene in Shakespeare's *Romeo and Juliet* where Romeo surprises Friar Laurence with the news that someone has caused him to forget his latest sweetheart, Rosaline. When the friar starts to lecture him on the fickleness of youth, Romeo's retort is that Laurence used to scold him for loving Rosaline. "For doting, not for loving, pupil mine," the kindly friar replies (Act II, scene iii, lines 81-82).

The distinction is one that is too seldom recognized. Friar Laurence understood the danger of wallowing in emotion, and particularly the way it can be an impediment to maturity. But the habit isn't limited to the young.

The heart-tugging wave of feeling that movies often aim for is a form of instant gratification, and the more tears the better. What is seductive in the process is that it makes us feel good about ourselves when we haven't *done* anything. It is so appealing to let this warm feeling be a substitute for active, involving love in our lives.

Sentimentality has long been a troubling temptation for Christians. It has become more common in recent decades as preachers and teachers have taken to television. Many of them have misled others with an appeal to warm feelings instead of the hard realities of redemption. The antidote is simply a better look at the Christ of the Bible.

Jesus is our ultimate pattern and example; every manifestation of love is to be tested by reference to his teaching. The bond of love between parents and children is one of the central themes of the Bible, as we have noted already. Nevertheless in Luke we find this startling dialogue:

> He said to another man, "Follow me."
> But the man replied, "Lord, first let me go and bury my father."
> Jesus said to him, "Let the dead bury their own dead, but you go and
>   proclaim the kingdom of God."
> Still another said, "I will follow you, Lord; but first let me go back and
>   say good-by to my family."

*Jesus replied, "No one who puts his hand to the plow and looks back
is fit for service in the kingdom of God."*
Luke 9:59-62 (Compare Matthew 8:19-22)

These words may seem harsh to us, but we dare not ignore them.
Elsewhere Jesus said, "Anyone who loves his father or mother more than
me is not worthy of me; anyone who loves his son or daughter more than
me is not worthy of me; and anyone who does not take his cross and
follow me is not worthy of me" (Matthew 10:37-38). The Christ who spoke
those words was no sentimentalist.

Some might object that these Scripture quotations offer a false emphasis. Indeed, Jesus himself gave us repeated instances of his tender regard
for individuals and his concern for family relationships. What I wish to
point out here is simply the importance of perspective—maintaining
priorities in our indulgence of feelings. Unfortunately, many people
adopt their priorities willy-nilly from the world of media entertainment.
What they know about "love" is what they gather from a steady diet of
TV and movie melodrama. Here is where a little discrimination and a
little hard-headed honesty will pay important dividends. Sentimentality
can be a drug; we can enjoy it profitably only if we know it for what it is.

Now I have to confess that I am a sentimentalist myself. I love the
novels of Dickens and Scott, the music of Verdi and Victor Herbert. I revel
in the uplifting effect of an old-fashioned musical like *The King and I* or
Camelot. But it is instructive to focus on the greatest artists in light of our
questions about sentimentality. Verdi, in some of his operas, wrote scene
after scene that "milked" the emotions of a father-daughter relationship.
But situations that in other hands might have become more soap than
opera became in his work the distillation of vital truths about love and
loyalty. And that was only one facet of Verdi's art. He poured his genius
into one masterpiece after another that was meant to reawaken us to the
Christian ideals of charity and forbearance, not to mention the civic ideals
of liberty, justice, and equality.

Even more to the point is the example of Dickens, since his work still
influences all our popular arts. Dickens has long been scorned by some
literary critics as the archsentimentalist. No creative artist has evoked
more tears than this man, with his irresistible handling of children in
distress—Little Nell, Oliver, Tiny Tim. But before we draw any conclu-

sions from this, let us not overlook the rest of the evidence. The work of Dickens lives—on the page and on the screen—because there is more to it than tears.

Dickens was a creative genius who could be captivated by his own characters, but he was also a man of blazing commitment to justice, and to the cause of human compassion. Over and over again he used the emotional grappling hook of pity in order to get people to care about specific wrongs in his society. (His considerable success is documented in the social history of nineteenth-century England.) Not only that, Dickens reveals a steady growth throughout his career *away* from excessive sentiment. His mature novels are notable for the way in which he analyzes the false or deceptive emotions of his heroes and heroines (see *Great Expectations* or *Bleak House*). *

Through the Tears and Smoke

In our involvement with entertainment, and especially movies, we need to develop a certain wariness of sentimentality. Unlike Dickens, the makers of today's popular entertainment are usually out to stimulate emotion for nothing more than its own sake. We gain much when we begin to enlarge our expectations of film and ask that it rise beyond the level of shallow manipulation. If we occasionally want to sample an old-fashioned tearjerker the option is always there; such a film can still be fun even when we recognize the emotional mechanics employed. But by asking for more in the movies, we learn to respond to those films that give honest and rational consideration to real love, rather than synthetic mush. Christian maturity demands nothing less.

Fortunately the VCR now offers us an unlimited selection of worthwhile film experiences. We can enjoy works of enduring value such as *Adam's Rib* (among other Tracey and Hepburn comedies), *The Best Years of Our Lives*, *Kramer vs. Kramer*, *Howard's End*, *Enchanted April*, and

*It is worthy of notice that Dickens had a unique influence on the origins of film technique. D. W. Griffith, often regarded as the most important figure in the development of the movies, was a great admirer of the writer. Griffith cited the novels of Dickens as the source of several devices that would become basic elements in the "language" of narrative film. The best example is the technique of parallel editing, in which we cut back and forth between two scenes unfolding at the same time—the heroine facing disaster in one location as the hero rides furiously (from miles away) to save her.

Shadowlands—all of which give mature, thoughtful treatment to marital love. Or we can be entertained by a strong tradition of intelligent romances that includes *The Shop Around the Corner; Alice Adams; Now, Voyager; I Know Where I'm Going;* and *Roman Holiday.*

We can find rewarding studies of family love in works as diverse as *Little Women, The Friendly Persuasion, A Raisin in the Sun, Marty, The Trip to Bountiful, Ordinary People, The Man in the Moon,* and *Lorenzo's Oil.* The remarkable *My Left Foot* and the more somber *I Never Sang for My Father* are modern family dramas that richly repay serious viewers.

Beyond these wait countless films that reflect an appreciation of love in a broader sense: caring, giving, supporting relationships between individuals who may differ widely in temperament and background. Some examples are *Captains Courageous, The Miracle Worker, The Elephant Man, Bang the Drum Slowly, Places in the Heart, The Killing Fields, 84 Charing Cross Road, Driving Miss Daisy,* and *Passion Fish.* These are love stories that respect the difficult aspects of love. The shallow sentimentality offered so often in commercial films will not be found here.

As we have seen, sentimentality is not the only means by which filmmakers manipulate viewers. Other categories of feeling than warmth and pity offer shortcuts to audience susceptibility. The commercial mainstream is clogged with action, sentimental melodrama, and comedy. The latter—usually billed as "irreverent" or "outrageous"—is glibly derived from racial, generational, or class resentments, and from sex. As in the action genres, there is little attention paid to character or values. Formula laws prevail here too: The next outrageous comedy will be a lot like the last.

Are we really entertained by these imitative commercial exercises? Are we helping our children to learn the appreciation of anything else? We and they need not be so limited, when the VCR can bring us Hollywood's finest achievements from the better part of a century. We have ready access to excellence: This is something Christians need to know, and to be reminded of. We need to be reminded because our judgment is under constant assault. Commercial and social forces push us to buy entertainment that is inferior, trite, and sometimes simply degenerate.

The most rewarding approach to today's entertainment market is twofold. We must prepare ourselves to reject the unworthy without regard to its popularity, and to claim the valuable without regard to its public neglect. We need to say an enthusiastic yes to the worthwhile *quiet* movie event, so often overlooked by the mass audience. And sometimes we have to say no to the trendy and the popular, even if it hurts.

Especially if it hurts. It is easy enough to exercise restraint when it comes to a wretched bit of pornography like *Sliver*. We take great satisfaction in avoiding a controversial work like *The Last Temptation of Christ*. But what about something that is genuinely popular? What if we refrained on principle from seeing *Beverly Hills Cop* or *Fatal Attraction*? That might be a real exercise of discipline.

The entertainment industry throws up enough smokescreens to blind all but the wariest consumers. Thus our greatest challenge is to maintain clear vision. Only in so doing can we make good choices for ourselves and our children. If Christians are not capable of this, who will be?

In a glut of screen products that are overheated, underdone, or distorted, it is up to us to mark again those distinctions that may be lost on the world at large. It is up to us to recognize the difference between love and sentimentality, between courage and bravado, to remember that while there are many ways of being strong, for Christians the only way is to be strong in love.

Notes to Chapter 7

1. Alistair Cooke, "Epitaph for a Tough Guy," *Atlantic*, May 1957, 33.

2. Laurence Perrine, *Sound and Sense: An Introduction to Poetry*, 4th ed. (New York: Harcourt Brace Jovanovich, 1973), 243.

"Daddy, have you been foolin'
with this VCR?"

Chapter 8

The Trouble
with Heroes

Ye have plowed wickedness, ye have reaped iniquity; ye have eaten the fruit of lies: because thou didst trust in thy way, in the multitude of thy mighty men.
Hosea 10:13 (KJV)

It was a crystal-clear afternoon in late winter. A small group of men, dressed in olive drab, was standing on a ridge, looking out over the plains of Oklahoma. We were on the practice range of the army's Artillery School at Fort Sill, and this was our initial "live" training as forward observers. We watched now for two trial rounds to hit somewhere in front of us—rounds I had called for. It was my first fire mission, and I had just managed to croak out the map coordinates that I hoped would put these rounds near the target.

There! Two puffs of smoke off to our right . . . *way* off to our right! My first calculation had been a disaster.

Near panic, I figured up a correction and called for the radical shift that seemed necessary: left 800 meters. Our instructor, a rawboned major who was himself a native Oklahoman, grinned mysteriously as we waited again.

This time the rounds hit directly behind the target.

What I should have done next was call for a moderate shift back toward us, to bracket the target beyond and before. That's the theory of fire adjustment. But for some reason I decided to gamble. I called for the full force of the battery with just a fifty-meter nudge: "Drop five-zero. *Fire for effect.*"

The major rolled his eyes and said, "Lieutenant Patterson has decided to John Wayne it."

A cold wind was blowing, but I felt a trickle of sweat down my back as we waited for the last time. Then the target disappeared in smoke as the rounds from six howitzers impacted around it. There were cheers from the rest of the platoon, and the major offered a good-natured quip about shaking out my trouser leg. I of course was elated; up until then my performance had been less than spectacular. And for several days my classmates kidded me with the nickname *John Wayne*.

This is a trivial example of the influence one movie star has had. It occurred in the late 60s, when Wayne was still alive and dominating the box office. The name and the image are not invoked so frequently now; other movie heroes have appeared, and some are thought of in much the same way. But John Wayne is not forgotten.

It may be that no movie personality will ever again have quite the same cultural significance. His name was known around the world. For several decades it came up routinely in discussions of what America stands for, or of sex roles in our changing society. That moment at Fort Sill was not the only time it was invoked during my army training. Whenever an instructor needed to caution trainees about taking shortcuts or operating equipment in a nonstandard, flamboyant manner, he would say, "Don't try to be John Wayne."

This all came back to me in the early weeks of 1991 as I watched news reports from Saudi Arabia. There, on my TV screen, army instructors warned the American soldiers of Operation Desert Storm: "Don't try to be like Rambo!"

More than anyone else, Wayne merits attention as the prototype movie hero in our time. Because he dominated the action genres of the immediate postwar era—the war movies and westerns—he established certain assumptions and expectations that still apply to screen heroics today. Eastwood, Stallone, Schwarzenegger, Harrison Ford, Mel Gibson—all are in some degree descendants of John Wayne.

Wayne's career, like most film careers, consisted of several distinct phases, in which different qualities predominated. In his early and middle years he took roles that offered positive models and/or excellent commentary on values. In later years the results are mixed at best.

When the star had become an icon, the effect and the influence were to raise serious questions.

Wayne's Early Prime

The performances that will best stand the test of time are probably those from Wayne's middle years, especially in the films of directors John Ford and Howard Hawks. Ford was able to put into clear relief the rugged strength and integrity of his star, but also to explore aspects of vulnerability that kept the hero human. In the Ford films Wayne plays distinctly fallible characters. In *Stagecoach*, for example (1939), he is perceived as a "kid" who needs to be helped toward a new start in life. In *The Long Voyage Home* (1940) he is so naive he is totally dependent on his shipmates to help him catch a boat home to Norway.

Angel and the Badman, despite the quaint title, offers an extremely likable sample of Wayne's work in the first half of his career. Filmed in 1947, it was the first movie that Wayne produced himself. He plays a gunfighter who falls under the influence of a Quaker family, especially the pretty daughter. There is no swaggering, but rather lots of sheepish exchanges with lovely Gail Russel. It is a B-western, done on a modest budget, and the plot is as improbable as most in the genre. Nevertheless the film offers a welcome twist on the revenge formula, and it is one of the most positive treatments of Quaker nonviolence that has reached the screen.

From start to finish the Christian ideal of loving one's enemy is treated with respect and not condescension. At the end, Wayne actually goes off to enter the peaceable life of the Quaker farmers, leaving his gun in the dust. A bystander then asks if he won't be needing it. The answer from the marshal is almost an exact paraphrase of Matthew 26:52—"Only a man that carries a gun ever needs one."

The Quiet Man (1952) offers the best illustration of the rounded human quality John Ford could elicit from Wayne. (It won a Best Director Oscar for Ford.) It is an unpretentious tale about a young American returning to his birthplace in Ireland. Wayne as an ex–prize fighter is strong and self-reliant and wins what he's after (Maureen O'Hara). But he also involves us in his character by being awkward, self-conscious, and continually frustrated. Most important of all, he needs the help of other people to deal effectively with the past that haunts him. The film as a whole is beautifully done—a winning production in every way.

Red River, filmed in 1948 by Howard Hawks, is one of the finest westerns ever made. It includes one of the Duke's most complex roles, and one of his best. The hero is a flawed, driven man, as we are reminded by the recurring comment from sidekick Walter Brennan: "You was wrong, Mister Dunson. . . ."

Wayne's second film with Howard Hawks, which did not come until 1959, is a memorable summation of the positive values in the Wayne hero. *Rio Bravo* is a typical Hawks film, with lots of camaraderie as four men learn to pull together toward a common goal, and the Hawks heroine (Angie Dickinson) proves her worth—and worthiness of the hero—by joining in their endeavor. Wayne commands the respect and loyalty of them all, but he does not domineer or bully. One wonders how Hawks ever persuaded him to do the scene where he sneaks up behind the cantankerous Brennan and plants a kiss on his head! As pure entertainment this film is surely a classic.

Remembering the Alamo

In 1960 John Wayne completed and released *The Alamo,* a project which had obsessed him for over a decade. He hoped that it would mark a transition for him from box-office star to major director. The Duke realized that advancing age would probably eliminate him from the sort of leading roles he had handled for thirty years. He had no illusions about his acting ability; he could not expect to branch out into more complex roles the way his friend James Stewart had done. (Imagine Wayne attempting to do the lead in *Harvey* or *Vertigo!*) He was pinning his hopes on a directing career.

But *The Alamo* brought as much disappointment as fulfillment. Though it attracted a considerable audience, the receipts did not come near to covering expenses. It lost millions, including a million or so of Wayne's own money. And it was followed by some annoying controversy. Wayne was thoroughly absorbed in the concerns of the cold war, and clearly intended for his magnum opus to be a lesson in patriotism. This met with a predictable variety of responses, pro and con. What raised a furious storm of resentment, however, was an unsubtle campaign for Academy

Awards which implied that those who did not vote for *The Alamo* (or its creators) were unpatriotic.

Wayne weathered the storm, but his production company was broke, and it was inconceivable that another studio would risk giving him a film to direct. This left him no alternative but to keep doing what he had always done—starring in westerns and action movies. He was fortunate to be involved just then in several highly successful films, such as *Rio Bravo* and *North to Alaska,* that kept his fans wanting more.

At this point the Duke must have realized that perhaps he *could* carry on indefinitely as the fearless two-fisted hero. Noting the success of his recent outings *other* than *The Alamo,* Wayne the movie star began to focus on the screen identity or *persona* that he would offer for the rest of his life. As the writers of a recent biography explain,

> Through his choice of material and with the aid of [writer] Jimmy Grant, he created a new and complex screen image. . . . In many respects, his new image was a recreation of himself, set in fictional worlds where the lines between good and evil, right and wrong were clearly defined and widely separated. It was this new image that firmly established him as a national institution and an ageless international superstar. . . .[1]

Now there would be no more experiments with foreign accents (as in *The Long Voyage Home),* no struggles with guilt, and certainly no dallying with Quaker principles.

New Lease for a Legend
The new image was polished elegantly by John Ford in his 1962 western, *The Man Who Shot Liberty Valance.* In this production James Stewart plays an idealist from "back East" who wants to tame the West with his law books. Wayne is the traditional frontier hero who puts his trust in his own strength and his own gun instead. The film is remarkable for the way the Wayne character is sentimentalized as the symbol of a vanishing era. (The future belongs to the lawyers, of course.) It is a case study in image construction, exploiting the contrast between the "weak" Stewart character and the indomitable Wayne.

Film scholar Robert Ray has written a fascinating analysis of how this contrast is achieved. He points out telling details like the costuming of Stewart in an apron as he becomes a waiter/dishwasher in a restaurant. Another device is the placing of Stewart in prone or helpless positions (on the floor, in the bed of a wagon) while the redoubtable Wayne rides "tall in the saddle" or stands erect over him. These striking visual images tell us which of them is the "real man": it is the strong, self-reliant one who knows how to take matters into his own hands. Stewart wins the girl, and Wayne ends his life a lonely, forgotten man. But director Ford has so romanticized the Wayne hero that it is he who wins the hearts of the audience.[2]

Ford was a master, and *Liberty Valance* is considered a masterpiece as a symbolic study of change in our developing nation. Unfortunately, the liberties Ford took in glorifying the Wayne hero were to be copied and expanded by lesser directors for the next two decades. The Wayne character would be more and more a stereotype, with less and less nuance.

In roistering epics such as *McClintock!* (1963), *The Sons of Katie Elder* (1965), or *El Dorado* (1967), audiences came to see John Wayne play John Wayne. They wanted to watch the two-fisted, invincible hero win out over the bad guys by being tougher and stronger. Wayne himself was determined to oblige them. However, in 1969 he provided a welcome change of pace with *True Grit*. At long last he played a delightful parody of his own persona . . . and won his only Oscar.

Aside from *True Grit* and its sequel, *Rooster Cogburn*, the Wayne films continued to rehash the same tired formula. The legend became more exaggerated, like a photo print left in the developing fluid too long. This was not a wholesome process, and the first to suffer from it may have been the Duke himself. He was in many ways an admirable man—sincere, honorable, and intensely patriotic. In choosing to make public his battle with cancer in the early 60s, he tried to serve as an inspiration to others who faced the same danger. But he was also an impulsive, driven man who could be hot-headed and vindictive. In some ways he was a prisoner of his own image.

Evidence of the problem appears in the testimony of another great director, Frank Capra. In his autobiography, Capra relates how he embarked on a project in the early 60s that would allow him to direct Wayne for the first time. He looked forward to it eagerly. However, shortly before filming was to begin in Europe, he was jolted by the discovery that he would have to deal with the personal writer (James Grant) who was attached to Wayne to see that his roles were always "appropriate." When Capra wanted to begin advance preparation of the script (prior to Wayne's arrival), Grant insisted that there was no need. As Grant explained,

> When he gets here, he and I will knock you out a screenplay in a week. All you gotta have in a John Wayne picture is a hoity-toity dame with [certain large endowments] . . . that Duke can throw over his knee and spank, and collection of jerks he can smash in the face every five minutes. In between you fill with gags, flags and chases.[3]

Capra decided to pass. He asked that some other director be called in to replace him.

In its final manifestation, the Wayne hero was a near-mythic symbol of strength and resolve. He was superior to every challenge and disdainful of those around him who displayed weakness, fear, or uncertainty. In 1968 Wayne did not hesitate to exploit this image in support of the Vietnam War. *The Green Berets*, which he helped to produce and direct, was a fervent endorsement of official U.S. policy.

It isn't hard to understand how, in those years of stress, millions of Americans would respond to the image. The Vietnam experience seemed to have thrown us off stride as a nation. The 60s and 70s were a time of confusion and uncertainty regarding our very identity. We became desperate to see ourselves as "winners." (This was the time when a sort of cult grew up around coach Vince Lombardi, and his dictum that "Winning isn't everything—it's the only thing," became a sacred text.) We had a gnawing fear of helplessness, though President Nixon had vowed to keep us from becoming a "pitiful, helpless giant."

In this atmosphere the Wayne persona reached the proportions of a superhero not capable of failure. Perhaps it was comforting for us to know that the Duke was still there to show us the way—just as he had shown us how to face down the Japs in *The Fighting Seabees* and *Sands of Iwo Jima*. Unfortunately, this is where the problems begin when we contemplate the Wayne myth from a Christian point of view.

What a Myth's Gotta Do

By the 1970s the name John Wayne registered in the American mind almost the way that earlier legendary names did—names like Davy Crockett, Paul Bunyan, John Henry. They all evoked imaginary persons (even if based on real figures such as Crockett) who performed feats of more than human skill or strength or courage. The various legends and tall tales connected with them served a valuable function in building the spirit of a frontier nation. And there is a dimension in which a movie legend such as Wayne can serve a similar valuable function—especially for a nation at war or in some other crisis.

Film critic Richard Schickel has pointed out the value to American society of an earlier action hero, Douglas Fairbanks. Fairbanks (Senior) was the first Hollywood superstar, well before that term had been invented. Handsome and athletic, he gained unprecedented popularity because his roles reflected the way Americans saw themselves. After World War I we were newcomers on the world stage. Beneath our cocky Yank facade, there was the hint of an inferiority complex with regard to our European neighbors. Douglas Fairbanks appeared in numerous films as a young man who at first looks naive and inept, but who at some crisis achieves a startling turnabout. He demonstrates unexpected pluck and daring, winning universal admiration in the end. It was a variation on the Horatio Alger theme, and America warmly embraced the hero who embodied it on the screen with such flair.[4]

Part of Fairbanks' charm was his ready smile, token of a healthy sense of fun. Similarly the early American heroes, especially in the frontier legends, all seem to have a delightful flavor of comedy about them. When people told stories about Paul Bunyan or Pecos Bill, they expected to get a laugh. The idea of Davy Crockett killing a bear as a toddler was probably the most fun for men who actually had to deal with bears and other wild creatures to survive. The exploits of such characters in taming the forces of nature are so exaggerated as to be hilarious. As much as anything, it was the element of humor in the tall tales that helped the pioneer face the all-too-real challenges of the frontier.

Those who want to create legends in post-frontier America could take a hint from the tall tales. A figure such as John Wayne achieves his greatest and most enduring value when the sense of fun is evident, not when he is taking himself too seriously as protector of the nation and its way of life.

One appealing feature of the Indiana Jones action-adventure series has been the element of tall-tale exaggeration—a sense of the ridiculous. These films feature an indomitable action hero that youngsters can cheer with abandon. At the same time they say to the mature audience, with a good-natured wink, "We all know this could never happen, but isn't it fun to pretend?" The impossible heroics of the later John Wayne films are not there just for fun. Rather, the audience is encouraged to believe they could be done, and that the world would be a better place if somebody were man enough to try them today.

Heroic Virtues and Christian Virtues

We do need heroes. We need them first as children to teach us courage and perseverance. In his fascinating study, *The Uses of Enchantment*, psychologist Bruno Bettelheim detailed the ways in which fairy tale heroes help growing children to deal with their emotions and establish positive values. The late Joseph Campbell gained a wide audience with his writings about the importance of myths and heroes in our age and in every other.

The subject is not new; it can be traced back to Plutarch and beyond. One of the first writers to analyze the phenomenon of the hero in depth was Thomas Carlyle. His collection of essays titled *On Heroes, Hero-Worship and the Heroic in History* was a popular work of the Victorian period. In these pieces Carlyle examines a variety of noted individuals from Socrates to Napoleon. The differences from one to another bear out the truth that there are many kinds of heroism.

No one should know better than Christians that there is more to life than courage, and more to courage than being tougher and stronger than everybody else. One of the heroes to whom Carlyle devotes his attention is Martin Luther. Christians and non-Christians alike picture Luther as a man of great strength, a bulldog of determination. Surprisingly, the attribute that Carlyle focuses on most particularly is Luther's warm, loving heart: "A most gentle heart withal, full of pity and love, as indeed the truly valiant heart ever is." Mere physical courage, Carlyle suggests, is hardly to be considered the preeminent virtue. After all, fear may be displaced in a number of ways. "There may be an absence of fear which arises from the absence of thought or affection, from the presence of hatred and stupid fury. We do not value the courage of the tiger highly."[5]

The qualities that John Wayne perfected so definitely in film after film were good qualities; there can be no mistake about that. But the characterization was so one-dimensional in his later films that only one category of virtues was offered: the hero displayed strength and self-assurance. Not much else seemed to matter. For the Christian who would place this figure on a pedestal (as much of the world did), a couple of questions call for attention: one, can we afford to narrow our focus to just one or two virtues; and two, are *these* the right virtues to stress? The Bible clearly indicates that the answer is *no* on both counts.

Paul's great formula for Christian character is found in Galatians 5:22 and 23: "The fruit of the Spirit is love, joy, peace, patience, kindness, goodness, faithfulness, gentleness and self-control." Notice, there is nothing said about being tougher than anybody else. There is no mention even of courage. Not that courage was a quality Paul disregarded. On the contrary, he makes much of valor and strength, and even suggests the analogy of athletic training with spiritual discipline (1 Corinthians 9:24-26).

The problem is basically a matter of what comes first. Choices become complicated, and the need for discernment greater, when we face attractive value alternatives. The world of films illustrates this perfectly. Its temptations are subtle. If the nation is swept up in admiration for a new hero—be it Wayne or Eastwood or Stallone—why not we also?

A key to maintaining the Christian perspective is to remember that civic virtues and spiritual virtues are not the same. The distinction is sometimes difficult for people in our society, which has been such a comfortable environment for Christianity. John Wayne was a splendid example of certain civic virtues—courage, loyalty, strength. We must honor such qualities, and indeed our dedication to them as free citizens should be almost second nature. *But what we are about as Christians is something else.* Rather, what God is making of us goes far beyond these traditional civic virtues. They, after all, were common to pagan societies before the Christianization of the West.

Jesus gave us a *new* commandment. It was clear and simple: that we love each other. Love is the one virtue that encompasses and inspires all others, the one without which all others are useless (see 1 Corinthians 13). What evidence of this paramount Christian virtue does the later western hero display? What inkling of it do we get from our more contemporary "mighty men"—the Eastwood cop, the Stallone warrior? As for the host of other macho avengers such as Arnold Schwarzenegger or Chuck Norris, the question is laughable.

To be sure, film writers occasionally attempt to set up a pretense of goodness in the action hero, a soft spot hidden beneath the tough exterior. At some point the script will flash us a signal that Mr. Macho has been hurt by the one he loved. *See* . . . he *would* be warm and caring if only fate had not dealt him such a blow! Or he has loved and lost. Even Dirty Harry, we learn in the first film of that series, had a wife who was torn from him by a brutal crime. Thus he wins instant sympathy and his cynicism is made "understandable."

In this connection the *Lethal Weapon* series represented a step forward from the usual run of police-action films. Mel Gibson and family man Danny Glover create characters more rounded and sympathetic than their predecessors in the genre. We must also give credit to Clint Eastwood for later work that undermines the Dirty Harry stereotype. His award-winning *Unforgiven* (1992) presents an earnest critique of the macho hero (though it falters when Eastwood the director can't let go of the revenge formula). In 1993's *In the Line of Fire* Eastwood portrays the most warm and appealing screen hero he has done to date—and the most fallible.

In the John Wayne annals, family sentiment is exploited in a variety of ways. In later films like *Big Jake* (1971), the Duke gets to bash the bad guys because an improbable story line has had them kill or kidnap a loved one (the revenge formula yet again). But these ties of kinship are an obvious plot device; the sentimentality is stuck on like a badly wrapped splint. In fact, a glaring feature of *Big Jake* is the way Wayne beats up his own sons when they dare to cross him.

Forgotten Traits of Heroic Character
There is an interesting contrast between Wayne and some other stars of his own generation. We might think first of James Stewart, some of whose films have so much to offer the Christian audience. But Stewart was not primarily an action/adventure hero, as Wayne always was. The characters he portrayed were human and real, not bigger than life.

A more instructive comparison can be drawn between Wayne and Gary Cooper, the original cowboy hero of the sound era. Cooper also lent his heroic presence to war films and romantic epics like *Beau Geste*. He revealed a broader acting range than Wayne, making an indelible impression in such comedies as *Mr. Deeds Goes to Town* and *Ball of Fire*. When he played the action hero he displayed a grace and humor that the Duke never found. Whether it was as the Virginian (in the granddaddy of modern westerns) or real life heroes such as Lou Gehrig and Alvin York, the Cooper character possessed the charm of humility—he could be embarrassed, could see himself looking ridiculous and still enjoy the joke. He could be provoked to give the villain a sock on the jaw, but it was always on principle, never to prove anything to himself.

Richard Schickel has written perceptively of the contrast between Cooper and Wayne, who he says "replaced Cooper as the symbolic repository of the traditional American heroic values." Schickel sums up the difference in these words:

> When the latter [Cooper] seemed nearly always to be trying to find a way of gracefully, peaceably fitting into an alien landscape or situation, bestirring himself reluctantly to action only when his patience and suppleness went unrewarded or scorned, the core of Wayne's character was his grumbling, often angry refusal from the outset to accept his circumstances. . . . As a tamer of the wilderness, of women, of his country's enemies, it was Wayne's habit simply to overpower them, beat them down with main strength.[6]

It was the combination of integrity *and humility* that made Cooper effective, and beloved. And success notwithstanding, it is the absence of humility that robs the Wayne character of grace and subtlety. Humility, it must be added, is a quality that Christians cannot ignore—not if they take the New Testament seriously. But it is the opposite phenomenon of sheer, prideful domination that made Wayne magnetic for so many viewers. The same overbearing strength—a strength that can exist only in fantasy—makes today's action heroes favorites in the world's eyes. And this is the dangerous aspect of such heroes for the Christian viewer.

To the extent that we admire a certain figure, we are usually drawn to emulate that figure. The reports of children who jump from windows or garage roofs in imitation of Superman do not simply record abnormal behavior. They represent a tendency we all share. It can be seen on any playground when some young person takes a basketball and says, "Watch, I'm gonna be Michael Jordan," or when a young woman dresses herself to look like Madonna. The same tendency was acknowledged by the army when its instructors warned us not to try to be like John Wayne—even as trainees today are warned not to imitate Rambo. None of us ever completely outgrows the effect.

The Christian who exalts the self-sufficient, domineering Wayne image is choosing a position fraught with confusion and inconsistency. The same goes for Stallone, Schwarzenegger, or whoever is next in the lineage. If we wish (openly or secretly) to be the tough, strong man as depicted in the action movie genre, we are going directly counter to what the Bible teaches. And this is not some marginal detail; it is a central doctrine of the Old and New Testaments. It is the lesson that Moses learned in exile, and that King Saul tragically failed to learn. It is the essence of the story of David and Goliath. It is eloquently expressed in the prayer of Hannah, the mother of Samuel: "My heart rejoiceth in the LORD, . . . He raiseth up the poor out of the dust. . . . He will keep the feet of His saints, and the wicked shall be silent in darkness; for by strength shall no man prevail" (1 Samuel 2:1-9, KJV). The psalmist echoes the theme over and over in the familiar words "The Lord is my strength."

The importance of humility, of the recognition of our utter dependence upon God, receives even greater stress in the New Testament. It is apparent in every scene from Jesus' ministry; perhaps that is why we are so ready to take it for granted. *Turn the other cheek?* Oh yes . . . he did say that, didn't he? When this occurs to us—if it ever does any more—we shrug, and go on posturing and feinting, still trying to prove to ourselves and others how strong we are, and falling under the spell of yet another worldly hero who specializes in overpowering others, either by his own strength or by the counterfeit strength of weapons.

For the Christian who is acquainted with the Epistles of Paul, today's macho role model has little to offer. Consider Paul's instructions to Timothy in 2 Timothy 2:24-25: "The Lord's servant must not quarrel; instead, he must be kind to everyone, able to teach, not resentful. Those who oppose him he must gently instruct, in the hope that God will grant them repentance leading them to a knowledge of the truth." Note that it is God who brings about repentance, not we.

More to the point is one of Paul's most personal confessions, the familiar reference in 2 Corinthians to an infirmity that he called his "thorn in the flesh." The insight Paul was to gain goes straight to the heart of our dilemma here. Paul relates that he asked the Lord three times to remove his burden,

> But he said to me, "My grace is sufficient for you, for my power is made perfect in weakness." . . . That is why, for Christ's sake, I delight in weaknesses, in insults, in hardships, in persecutions, in difficulties. For when I am weak, then I am strong.
>
> 2 Corinthians 12:9-10

Paul is saying things that aren't fashionable in today's world. But we cannot keep ignoring him. It is for us to choose between the truth of our historic faith and the popular lie of contemporary culture.

The world will always be ready to exalt the prideful "mighty man" portrayed by Wayne or one of his heirs. But if we Christians become enthralled, we are falling into a trap. To the degree that we admire these heroes we will be tempted to see our lives in the too-simplified terms that action movies insist on. Filmmakers know how to press all the right buttons to get the desired emotional response from an audience. They invariably set up a conflict between the hero and one or more opponents who are irredeemably bad. Life is neatly divided; it's them against us. And so the temptation comes to think of our own conflicts in these simple terms, to expect simple solutions based on power. We are subtly persuaded that the best way to prepare for life's problems is to *make ourselves stronger*—forgetting the message of the Bible, that it is God alone who gives strength.

When we take vicarious satisfaction in the exploits of a Big Jake, a Dirty Harry, or a Rambo, we are tuning to a dangerous moral wavelength. If trouble arises in our dealings with others we may hear a murmur in the back of our minds that "this enemy of mine needs to be taught a lesson." If we can't give him a punch in the mouth, we can at least deliver a swift verbal knockdown. Just like John Wayne. Just like Arnold. But when we yield to this impulse, Christian behavior goes out the window. The image of the invincible movie hero is leading us away from Christ.

Let us always be on the lookout for another Gary Cooper, another Jimmy Stewart. (Recent would-be heirs such as Kevin Costner have had only limited success.) Otherwise we must leave the subject of the action hero with an urgent word of caution. The world may make idols of the Duke, of Eastwood, Stallone, or Schwarzenegger. The Christian must not, no matter what lurid evils they oppose, no matter what revered flags or symbols they embrace. If they distort our perception of who we are, or of the One we serve, they are dangerous idols indeed.

For adult Christians it boils down to this: How much do we need a hero if we have a Savior?

Notes to Chapter 8

1. Donald Shepherd and Robert Slatzer with Dave Grayson, *Duke: The Life and Times of John Wayne* (Garden City, New York: Doubleday, 1985), 256.

2. Robert B. Ray, *A Certain Tendency of the Hollywood Cinema, 1930–1980* (Princeton, New Jersey: Princeton University Press, 1985), 217–28.

3. Frank Capra, *The Name Above the Title* (New York: Vintage Books, a division of Random House, 1985), 489–90.

4. Richard Schickel, *Schickel on Film* (New York: William Morrow and Company, 1989), 151.

5. Thomas Carlyle, *On Heroes, Hero-Worship and the Heroic in History,* originally published 1841, The World's Classics (London: Oxford University Press, 1965), 184.

6. Schickel, 197.

Chapter 9

Sex

People who want to get rich fall into temptation and a trap and into many foolish and harmful desires that plunge men into ruin and destruction. . . . For the love of money is a root of all kinds of evil.
1 Timothy 6:9-10

"This is all very good, but I hope you're going to say something about sex."

So said a friend who had just read some early chapters of this book in manuscript. Her comment did not surprise me. She is the mother of two teenage sons, and she is a committed Christian. Believers in every age have faced stern challenges, but the challenge of guiding young people into adult life today must rank as one of the toughest ever. At the heart of this challenge, making it more perplexing every year, is the potentially explosive matter of sexual behavior. My friend had a right to her concern.

The response was affirmative, of course: There would be "something about sex." I may have said it with a sigh, because her comment reminded me of the difficulties that face anyone who takes up the subject. A lot of people will be unhappy with any views on sex that do not exactly coincide with their own. When so many other important things need to be said about movies, the temptation is strong to avoid the sex issue and assume that everyone already has his mind made up anyway.

But sex has too great an impact on popular culture to be passed over. Although it has been referred to in nearly every chapter of this book, there are certain more specific observations that need to be made.

We can begin by taking note of something that is well known but often overlooked: Movies have much in common with our dreams. To sit in a theater while the lights go down and then let the brilliant images remove us from awareness of the real world is to simulate the escape function of sleep and dreams. As dreams are a primary outlet for sexual concerns, it is not surprising that movies lend themselves to the expression of sexual themes as well. There have always been filmmakers eager to exploit this dimension, just as there have been conscientious and idealistic filmmakers.

Because the movie camera provides an intimate view of strangers who are at once human beings and insubstantial flickers of light, it encourages a natural curiosity. If we happen to be walking past a strange house at night and suddenly see someone in the window, most of us will keep looking momentarily. The more mature we are, the more quickly we will remove ourselves from the situation. If we observe for a moment and pass on, no harm has been done.

Movies allow us to do the same thing, but with a more complete impunity because it is impossible that we could ever meet or relate to the persons spied upon. These "persons" do not really exist. Yet we still experience the secret pleasure of looking in on the intimate lives of others while remaining unseen. "Remember, they're *peeking* at you," said Charlie Chaplin to the actors in his productions.[1]

The privilege of invisibility brings with it a natural desire to make the most of the opportunity: Our first impulse is to look for those things we would not get to see under ordinary circumstances. To say that such curiosity is natural is not to say that it is innocent. But this does shed light on the temptation for filmmakers to exploit more or less taboo subjects.

I have suggested that the peeking experience is harmless when governed by a mature self-restraint. The innocent pedestrian turns and walks on. The movie audience is another matter; here the maturity and restraint must be found in the person behind the camera. The question of degree is significant: A mere glimpse of nudity is far different from the portrayal of the sex act that some movies now offer. Unfortunately, copulation is almost commonplace in films for adults and even teenagers. In most instances it is unnecessary and exploitative—merely there to sell tickets. In this form it has great potential for harm to impressionable viewers.

But we cannot deny that the general audience today is highly knowledgeable with regard to sex and takes it for granted as earlier audiences could not have done. Even the most conscientious filmmaker must communicate with the audience of his own time, and not some other. Given this situation, we must consider the possibility that in certain films, scenes that include simulated sex are justifiable. The filming of such scenes, and our experience of them, can be defended on the basis of a few clear conditions: 1) the maturity (not merely the age) of the audience, 2) the artistic purpose of the filmmaker, and 3) the taste that is displayed in the handling of the scene. The first of these is our own affair entirely; the last two we should be capable of judging on the evidence.

The filmmaker who is a huckster leads his audience to the bedroom because he is interested in the *audience's* lust and excitement. The filmmaker who is a serious artist leads us to the bedroom because he is interested in the *characters* and their experience of life in all its joy and pain. The difference is essential for Christian viewers.

What Makes the World Go Round
Unfortunately it is the hucksters who predominate in screen entertainment today. A naive observer from another planet could easily make one generalization about contemporary culture—sex sells. Many Christians waste valuable energy and treadware on the vocal cords by missing the implications of this phrase. They react to the pervasiveness of sex, and overlook the importance of the selling. That is why I included the verses from 1 Timothy as the epigraph for this chapter. Sex is a powerful element in modern life, but greed, its silent partner, is just as powerful.

Sex has come to be used without restraint in the selling of our products, including entertainment. Successful selling is the keystone of our way of life, and whatever aids the process acquires a status of immunity from question. Whenever a thing becomes good for business, objections that might once have been heeded no longer have any effect. It is no coincidence that the ascendancy of sex in popular culture came at the same time as the rise of the advertising industry, with its particular concentration in television.

Selling is what modern America is about, and those in the entertainment industry know it better than anyone else. Pity the young actress of today who objects to performing in the nude. She has to deal with the fact that most movies are made only to generate profits, and they are calculated to do so on the basis of a few inelegant formulas. What roles are there for a starlet who will not routinely shed her clothing to pump up the audience's pulse rate? (I sometimes wonder how a Katherine Hepburn or a Margaret Sullivan would get her start today!)

Some performers have found a way to cling to a pretense of modesty: the steamy sex scenes are filmed with a stand-in, and the movie's publicity makes it known that the ladylike star was not tarnished by the proceedings. This pretense is accepted by the public, who then admire the "high standards" of the star. There is no question of her refusing to do the *film*, since we all know that sex is required for films to make money. Having movies without sex would be like having pro football games without seminude cheerleaders, or car ads without seductive poses and smouldering looks. How would people make any money *that* way?

The runaway hit of 1990, *Pretty Woman*, illustrates today's commercial/cultural marriage of money and sex. The film is a slick amalgamation of components from earlier sources such as *Pygmalion* (or *My Fair Lady*) and the story of Cinderella. It pushes tried and true buttons of audience sympathy by setting up a number of cliché conflicts: the poor girl versus the snobs, the free and natural (she) versus the uptight and repressed (he), the sensitive man versus the male chauvinist pig. There is nothing too hard for the mass audience to assimilate at once.

The movie's appeal is founded on wish-fulfillment, and the wishes it addresses are basically two—money and sex. What male in the audience would not want to possess more money than he could count *and* a beautiful young girl who is an artful (if automatic) sex partner? What woman in the audience can resist the idea of being swept up into the life of a dark and handsome lover with more money than he can count? (And there is the added feature that Mr. Rich-and-Handsome is also a shy, sensitive "modern" male.) If that isn't enough, throw in a sequence where the heroine spends a day buying extravagant clothes with his credit, looking very much like a model and not much like a runaway-turned-prostitute. Peddling such fantasies as this, the film reaches new heights in vicarious gratification.

Pretty Woman is easy to enjoy. The two leads play well in their situations, especially Julia Roberts as the heroine. The problem is the hypocrisy: There are just too many implicit lies regarding sex and money. To begin with, there is the heroine who is a prostitute, but still somehow an innocent, *unspoiled* prostitute! She is physically stunning, and she is ready, willing, and able to "perform" in bed. The film exploits the notion of sex at a professional level of skill while it ignores the realities of prostitution.

The fantasy menu for the female audience may be more pernicious. Julia Roberts come into possession of a dream life and a dream wardrobe almost the way people do on game shows. But the game she plays to win her fortune is the sex game. If she hadn't been working the sidewalk, her prince charming would never have snatched her up and carried her away.

Of course the hero's wealth has complicated his life. Moviemakers understand that the audience *thinks* it knows money can't buy happiness. But wait! What if the fresh, fun-loving heroine teaches him how to enjoy life in spite of being rich? Then they can both be rich *and* happy—and have great sex all the time.

How can such a mishmash of fantasies help young men or women to cultivate desirable, realistic self-images? How can it help them to focus on values that are eternal, or goals that are truly satisfying? Christians know that it cannot. Yet many of us will respond to the film uncritically along with the rest of the public. And such is the complacency of the entertainment industry that in May of 1991 there were newspaper ads touting the *Pretty Woman* video as the perfect Mother's Day gift!

Until Christians start to examine the subtle interdependence of sex and greed, we will never begin to comprehend the place of sex in our culture.[2] Our hand-wringing about sex in the movies and on TV will be as ineffectual as it has indeed been for the past twenty years.

It would be easy enough to fill page after page with a diatribe on sex in the movies. It would be easy to find quotes—good ones, too—from all sorts of authorities that reinforce our Christian concerns. Many people in the movie world itself have expressed their dismay. But there is not much point in further lamentation or evidence-gathering. We don't need to describe the problem; we need to get at some solutions for the individual Christian.

Like our discussion of profanity, this will largely boil down to a question of discernment. It cannot be a matter of easy simplifications. Where everything is divided into neat, obvious elements of black or white, discernment is not a factor. That is not the case with sex and movies. Certain clear-cut categories of good and bad exist, but they are not the only categories. Many choices offer themselves that are not clear cut. If we limit ourselves to simple rules for giving thumbs up or thumbs down on a movie, we leave ourselves only meager opportunities for reward. When we make evaluations, we must do so on the basis of our gospel in its completeness, not just a hasty application of Scripture quotes. The same Lord who created us created sex; he did not intend for us either to treat it casually or to cling to a childish ignorance about it.

The Bible—Excuse or Example?

There is a tired argument that often surfaces in discussions of sex and entertainment. Someone will say with an air of sophistication, "After all, the Bible is full of sex." The implication is that Christians need not make such a fuss about it. Those who say this are half right: Sex does appear in the Bible, and it has great significance there. But when we are evaluating contemporary entertainment, the only meaningful comparison will feature the manner and the situations in which biblical writers treat sex.

The biblical references to sex are not there to titillate and provoke. On the other hand, biblical writers are neither squeamish nor shy in the matter. While the Old Testament reports examples of appalling sexual behavior, the narrative pulls no punches and adds no hype. These are cases where the lust and cruelty of mankind are reported honestly—and this is the way we must expect the honest filmmaker to report such things.

The Bible records many kinds of sexual encounters, not just the sensational incidents of rape and incest. The story of Joseph and Potiphar's wife is one of temptation and its noble resistance by the hero. It is rendered in unusual detail; Genesis chapter 39 takes twenty verses to develop this soap-opera scenario of desire, frustration, and duplicity. The scene is carefully set, the dialogue presented at length. The writer clearly wants to draw us into the situation as fully as he can, for only then can we sympathize sufficiently with the hero to recognize the cost of his struggle. Even so must the filmmaker offer realistic details if he wishes to register the moral struggles of his characters.

Biblical writers can be more than just matter-of-fact in dealing with sex. In 2 Samuel, when we are told the story of David's terrible sin with Bathsheba, the writer makes sure that we picture the moments of temptation vividly. We are told that "from the roof he saw a woman washing herself; and the woman was very beautiful to look upon" (2 Samuel 11:2, KJV). The modern film artist, recounting such a scene, would have no meaningful alternative but to picture the woman's beauty as David saw it—naked in the moonlight.

One of the most beautiful stories in the Bible is that of Naomi, Ruth, and Boaz. The friendship and eventual marriage of the latter make up a charming romance, and it includes a definite sexual dimension. Furthermore, the story offers an instance of sex as it is recognized candidly and honored as the ordained gift of God.

The two central characters, Ruth and Boaz, are exemplary and appealing persons. The stratagem suggested by Naomi—coming to Boaz in the night after he has enjoyed his food and drink—is certainly honored in the telling. If anyone were blind enough to insist that this vignette deals only with legalities and the need for housing, the story would suffer irreparably. It does have to do with the fulfillment of legal obligations. But far more than this, it is a multidimensional love story, in which Naomi's care for her daughter-in-law remains prominent. And besides this, it is about sex, whatever we assume the two principals did or did not do that night on the threshing floor. Why else would Naomi be instructing Ruth to wash and perfume herself and put on her best clothes, and then to wait till after the feasting and drinking to insinuate herself into the presence of Boaz (Ruth 3:3)?

The planning, the hoping, and the fulfillment of plans and hopes, all come about in the context of God's unfailing love for his children. It is a remarkable story, not least for giving us as leading characters a mature man and woman who behave with unwavering respect and tenderness toward each other.

While taking note of sex in a wholesome and positive biblical setting, we should mention the Song of Songs, or Song of Solomon. This unique book is sadly taken for granted by various groups of readers, often for opposite reasons. Some mention the Song of Songs with a knowing smile, as if to say that the biblical writer is actually a forerunner of the hippie movement. These people probably haven't read the book, or have been tipped off to some of the "juicy" sections, which they have read without giving much thought to the entire work. In the opposite corner, and equally misguided, is the group that finishes off any reference to the Song of Songs with the explanation that "it's all symbolic" and only serves as some kind of code message about the church being the bride of Christ.

Symbolic the book certainly is, but to conclude that the sexual dimension is therefore neutralized is absurd. The symbolism is powerful only if the things used as symbols are real. Here, when we read attentively, we find imagery of the human body so vivid it is almost startling (as in chapters 7 and 8). There is no stumbling or mumbling, not a hint of embarrassment. Whatever else this writing is intended to do, it serves to celebrate the body as it was ordained by the Creator to be enjoyed.

Fine, you say, but this is off the subject. Beautiful poetry about physical love is one thing; movies are something else. The Song of Songs is safe in the middle of the Bible, and few people are going to read it anyway. That's a far different matter from filling up a movie screen with bodies, from putting desire and consummation in front of the camera.

Here again the watchword for mature Christians is the intention of the artist. The biblical passages we have examined are models of the proper relationship between purpose and handling. There are moments when nudity can have a positive value in a serious film for adults. To make this judgment in the case of a given film we must consider what the movie *as a whole* is telling us about ourselves and our world. Does the director use this exposure of the body discreetly to illuminate the character or state of mind of the persons in the story, or does he cause the camera to linger voluptuously and tease our senses? There are plenty of both kinds of director.

Putting Sex at the Center

Unfortunately, the task of discrimination is not always complete with a simple division of the artists from the exploiters, the sincere from the cynical. We must also take into account the treatment of sex that is simply misguided. Our society has invested such importance in the concept of sexual pleasure (with the encouragement of a new priestly class in the field of psychoanalysis) that sex receives uncritical reverence from many sincere, well-intentioned people. In the nineteenth century, sex may have been a source of unwarranted fear and confusion. In our time it has gained the exalted status of the sacred cow. Sex is one of the few absolutes we acknowledge: "Everybody knows" that sexual gratification is essential to the individual's well-being; "everybody knows" how wrong it is to harbor fears and inhibitions about sex. This is clearly evident in our anguished public discourse about AIDS.

But a little enlightenment can be a dangerous thing. In this age of sex as an absolute, conscientious filmmakers may offer an ill-considered treatment of sex in otherwise excellent films. The problem is compounded when popular opinion likewise assumes that these films treat sex in a wholesome manner. Once again Christian viewers will face the necessity of thinking for themselves.

An example is *Moonstruck,* the popular 1987 comedy by Norman Jewison. From a number of standpoints this is a delightful movie. It features fine acting, and it gives us a thoughtful, generous-spirited evaluation of modern family relationships. The story involves the familiar predicament of a character engaged to the "wrong" partner (compare *Holiday* or *I Know Where I'm Going.)* The plot amounts to the discovery and the claiming of the right mate. Cher, who is engaged to one man (played by Danny Aiello), finds that she is much better suited to his brother (Nicholas Cage).

We know that Cher and Cage belong together because of what they have in common—intelligence, sensitivity, passionate natures, etc. But the obvious evidence of their personalities is not enough for director Jewison. He throws these two headlong into a sexual encounter on their first meeting. To be sure, the rush into intimacy is not unlikely in a fiction about two overwrought and impressionable people. But Jewison insists on a second sexual experience following directly on the confusion and remorse that attend the first. At this point the sex weighs down and distorts the film.

A great story can often be found in persons who come to know who they are and then recognize in another the qualities that best complement their own. This is always the most valuable kind of love story. *Moonstruck* has all the elements of such a story. But instead of letting the lovers make their choice based on mutual awareness and recognition, it needlessly imposes sex as the defining factor. Although we know it already because of *who they are,* the film redundantly presents "great sex" as the guarantee that the lovers are made for each other. *Working Girl* (1988) is remarkably similar in its misapplication of sex to a finding-the-right-mate formula.

The same problem occurs in another highly popular film of 1988, *Bull Durham.* The story line again features lovers (Susan Sarandon and Kevin Costner) who are obviously right for each other, but who take their time in coming to the realization. Here again we follow two people who are exceptional (in the setting) for their maturity and intelligence. The character of the woman must develop emotionally as she outgrows her promiscuous past and commits herself to the man who is right for her. Nevertheless, at the end of the film what binds our maturing heroine to the right man is the same kind of sexual extravaganza that she used to enjoy with the immature hunks. The appeal to sex as the real defining element in a relationship is more gratuitous here than it is in *Moonstruck* or *Working Girl*.

In these and other well-regarded films, the Christian will watch with a sharper critical eye than the public at large. It is possible to appreciate various commendable aspects of a film while regretting a blurred moral focus in regard to sex. However, to render this kind of careful judgment requires skill and concentration. It is not for lazy thinkers.

We have seen that films with a significant sexual element can fall into at least three categories: 1) those that involve sex for valid reasons and treat it with mature discretion, 2) those that are misguided or unthinking in the treatment of sex, and 3) those that deliberately exploit sex. Clearly, a sexual encounter in a film may or may not be an evil thing. It depends on the overall purpose of the film and the filmmaker's integrity in fulfilling that purpose.

Fortunately we need not be helpless or uninformed when dealing with the question of integrity. Everyone in movies is leaving a record with each project he or she takes on. With as much reporting as there is these days, we can almost always arm ourselves with useful information about the creators of a film, particularly in regard to their motivations. We can usually judge them by their past work—their fruits, no less. A Richard Attenborough, a Bruce Beresford, or a Roland Joffe is not likely to serve up a shallow, exploitative movie. There are plenty of directors, past and present, from Howard Hughes to John Derek, who merit the opposite expectation. But singling out the unworthy is far less important for us than identifying and claiming the worthy.

Some contemporary movies do employ sex and nudity in a tasteful, valid manner. One such film is *Witness* (1985). This is not a great film, but it is a serious, well-intentioned one that may be recommended highly to adult Christians. The central character, played by Harrison Ford, is a man who experiences a modern conflict of values. He is in flight from the violent, decaying city and takes refuge among simple and pious Amish farmers of rural Pennsylvania. Of course his dilemma, as he gains an increasing awareness of what Amish life represents, finds its focus in his attachment to a beautiful young Amish widow (Kelly McGillis).

Their hesitant, largely unspoken attraction reaches a sudden crisis when he inadvertently discovers her bathing in an outbuilding. These two desire each other—we already know that—and she responds to the circumstances by standing still, letting her arms fall to her sides, her breasts revealed without shame. The man gazes at her through the door, but only for a moment. With a look of ineffable regret he turns and disappears into the darkness.

This encounter is memorable for the values it affirms. Two persons are struggling with their desires and emotions, not so much tempted to vice as responding to the appeal of something good but unwise. With mature judgment, Harrison Ford makes the decision to refuse his opportunity; he recognizes that they cannot share life contentedly given the difference in their backgrounds.

The two of them respect each other too much to accept the reckless indulgence that is today's norm. The young woman's actions do not indicate an abandonment of principle. In leaving herself open to his gaze she is not displaying weakness, but rather making the choice to commit herself to him regardless of the obstacles. In that moment of the interrupted bath (and perhaps she knew that he might find her there) she was saying, "Yes, I am willing to take the risk of leaving all I have been." It is a moment of great courage on her part—a fact not lost on her admirer. But he has made the difficult choice, and at the end he returns to his world and leaves her to her own—a melancholy but honest conclusion.

If this brief occurrence of nudity had been left out, the film would have been weakened. We care about these people. We share their uncertainty and torment over which way to proceed. The glimpse we get of her radiant beauty allows us to feel with the hero the emotional magnitude of the dilemma. And it causes us to recognize the extent of his maturity and his consideration for her in mastering his desire and giving her up.

Some people may disagree that the nudity here served to enhance the film. They would say we can understand just as clearly what is going on if we aren't shown the offending flesh. I doubt it. We have to live in our own time, and ours is a day when much of the body is commonly displayed in public. You don't even have to go to a beach. You can visit any mall or supermarket and see bare flesh in a way another decade could not have comprehended (at least in the European tradition). Modern society has largely dispensed with modesty, and the filmmaker must take us as he finds us.

This is not to deny that an erotic mood can be generated between persons who are fully clothed. The movies offer abundant evidence that it can. (Look at Humphrey Bogart and Lauren Bacall in *To Have and Have Not*, or Myrna Loy and Fredric March as the long-separated husband and wife in *The Best Years of Our Lives*.) But if a film is dealing with men and women in the 1990s, it is hardly fair to rule out the option of nudity.

As we have seen, nudity is not the only problem we must consider. It may now be the least troubling aspect of sex in films.

A Familiar Guideline
In an earlier chapter I stated that Christians must have a cautious attitude about sentimentality because we understand the importance of love. The same principle applies to the question of sex. The best way to make a judgment in this regard is to ask what relationship exists between love (as Christians understand it) and the film's treatment of sex. The question is neither complicated nor abstract.

Most adults can determine when a sex scene is presented only to entice the lust of the audience and when it serves to deepen our understanding of the characters and their situation. Most of the sex that occupies the first category has no essential connection to the plot or to character development. It does not represent love between the participants. Furthermore, the treatment does not reflect any compassion on the part of the film-maker for his characters.

On the other hand, there are films for adults in which the depiction of the sex act is just the opposite. The behavior flows naturally from a genuine love; sex is an essential expression of the way the characters relate. Many times the serious handling of characters who love is revealed in a restrained, unsentimental approach to physical intimacy. This tells us that the filmmaker is a responsible artist who cares for the persons in his story. It is a manifestation of the love that is necessary for real art (an idea we shall examine further in the next chapter).

Christians understand that among other things, love is discipline. The best films that incorporate lovemaking do so with the discipline of restraint and understatement. The 1967 feature *Bonnie and Clyde* is a modern classic that incorporates much raw violence and some nudity. The plot requires a love scene in which the two leading characters consummate their relationship, and Clyde Barrow overcomes the problem of impotence. When this moment arrives in the film, all that we are shown directly is an ardent kiss. The director cuts away to the empty field in which the couple lie, and the sequence works perfectly well to tell us that their love has found physical expression. This kind of film art has everything to do with sexuality, but nothing to do with selling sex.

Bonnie and Clyde did not include a scene of actual lovemaking because none was necessary. But an equally serious and compassionate film might do so and not deserve rejection by mature Christians. A number of distinguished foreign films such as *The Return of Martin Guerre* and *Passione d'Amore* have incorporated sex scenes (necessary to the plot) in a sensible, artistically valid fashion. The same is true of certain American films. Steven Spielberg's *The Color Purple* has some glaring weaknesses, but it is the product of earnest, loving endeavor by Spielberg and his collaborators. The painful and even heartbreaking sexual encounters of the heroine are crucial to the unfolding of the story. Examples like this may be few and far between, but they do exist.

The mere inclusion of sex in a film is not wrong; lying about the ultimate meaning of sex is. This is what separates films like *Pretty Woman* and *Bull Durham* from those in the category of *Bonnie and Clyde* or *The Color Purple*.

While asserting that love must determine the place of sex in a film, we must recognize that this is a demanding principle. It is often abused by those who wish to make it an excuse for exploitation. Filmmakers who peddle sex almost always claim to do so in the name of love, or at least "romance." Thus the crucial premise is a mature comprehension of love. Such a comprehension has never been more rare than it is today. Watch a few hours of TV on any given night for proof. Listen to the teenager protesting to worried parents that "we really love each other." Listen to the sophistry of the divorce lawyers.

Mature judgment is the leavening agent that is essential when young people are struggling with their feelings and desires. Maturity is likewise the key to a just appreciation of sexuality in art. When the viewer is a child (of whatever age—thirteen or thirty), exposure to sexual content on screen will not be wholesome. But for mature Christians, the thoughtful treatment of sexual themes can be of great value.

I indicated earlier in this chapter that it would offer no simple answers. The question of what we should be comfortable with in regard to sex is far too complex. Movie morality will always be a subject of concern and probably frustration for Christians. But we need not despair; God does not leave us helpless in the face of any challenge. If we resolve to approach the questions with determination and prayerful confidence (along with a little common sense), we can find effective solutions.

Notes to Chapter 9

1. Leslie Halliwell, *Halliwell's Filmgoer's and Video Viewer's Companion,* ed. John Walker, 10th ed., (New York: HarperCollins, 1993), 4.

2. A good starting point is Mark Crispin Miller's essay "End of Story," which comprises the segment on advertising in *Seeing Through Movies,* ed. Mark Crispin Miller (New York: Pantheon Books, 1990). An even better place to start is Matthew, chapter 6.

Chapter 10

Art and
Redemption

*And David's anger was greatly kindled against the man; and he said to Nathan,
As the LORD liveth, the man that hath done this thing shall surely die.*

And Nathan said to David, Thou art the man.

2 Samuel 12:5, 7 (KJV)

There have always been thoughtful, morally responsible filmmakers who
see their work as a means of expressing important truths. Like Dickens,
some have even tried to use their medium to bring about the righting of
wrongs. But others scoff at the idea of doing good with movies and
ridicule or dismiss those who are guilty of such folly. "If you want to send
a message, call Western Union" is the traditional putdown of serious
intentions in film.

While people in the business have disagreed over the purpose of
movies, the public has been ambivalent or confused. Whenever movies
are mentioned as a vehicle for ideas or insight, whenever they are
considered as something other than pure entertainment, the word *art*
seems to intrude. This makes for trouble. Before we know it we are
confronting the phrase "film art" (or worse, "cinema art"), which calls to
mind incomprehensible foreign films where someone is always dreaming
something and the lens keeps distorting the images. If the phrase is
reversed we have "art film," which suggests pornography and triple Xs.

Against this background it is not surprising that some filmmakers
appear embarrassed about their moral seriousness and their artistic
aspirations. Movie stars typically make light of what they do, with

comments like "It beats working." Directors portray themselves as unpretentious hacks instead of idealists or intellectuals. John Ford, the most revered of all American directors, once told an interviewer, "I have never thought about what I was doing in terms of art. . . . To me, it was always a job—which I enjoyed tremendously—and that's it."[1]

Thus a strong Hollywood tradition encourages the view that movies are an ephemeral consumer product, not to be taken seriously. If we Christians follow this line of thinking, we are probably in the majority. We are also wrong, and for us the misconception can be a severe handicap. It can cut us off from one of the best resources to make us more fully aware of ourselves and of our neighbors.

Christians who spend time and money on movies owe it to themselves—and to the God they serve—to invest that time thoughtfully. This means we have to deal with movies as a serious activity. It means that individual movies are to be sought out for more than mere diversion. Some movies can be enjoyed as light entertainment, for relaxation and escape, but movies in general must be viewed as more than a recreational pastime. At their best movies have the power to touch us, to enlighten us, to *change* us. For that reason they are to be cherished. And for that reason they must be approached with discretion.

Who should be more discerning in his or her movie preferences than today's Christian? The sad fact is that many of us have been satisfied to drift with the herd in our choices and enthusiasms. But our culture has reached a point where we cannot keep drifting from one popular TV show to the next, from one trendy movie to the next, and still lead a life committed to the Christ of the New Testament.

We cannot leave the most nourishing screen fare to better-informed viewers while we choose mediocrity along with an undiscriminating majority. That is like being at a banquet and missing the main course because we stayed in the lobby munching on the crackers and dip. Christians need the meat and vegetables prepared by our most serious creative talents, not cultural junk food.

Perhaps we are influenced by a suspicion of Hollywood. Movies have been denounced from the pulpit at various times and places throughout the century. Somehow this remains in the back of our minds. At the same time Christian parents who themselves did not believe in going to movies have seen their children become regular viewers.

Now more and more of us are seeing films at home with the VCR. But some of us still worry that it may be wrong to enjoy a movie at all. And at this point it is easy to latch onto a curious psychological defense: If there is an element of wickedness inherent in films, we can render it harmless *if we refuse to take them seriously*. We can guard our innocence by claiming that a movie doesn't mean anything anyway.

Unfortunately, this way of viewing movies leaves us vulnerable to the assault of mediocrity. We join the bandwagon for a superficial box-office hit, while we neglect more challenging films that might pay real dividends in our Christian awareness.

The purpose of this chapter is to call attention to our need for serious films, and to the value of film art for the Christian imagination. Movies have been serious, and movies have been art, since the days of D.W. Griffith. Like any other medium, they can be appraised in terms of what they are about and how they are made. While we will focus more of our attention on content than on craft, we will not forget that in any art the thing that is said cannot be considered separately from *how* it is said. A helpful discussion of this principle can be found in Leland Ryken's *The Liberated Imagination: Thinking Christianly about the Arts* (chapter 3 and elsewhere). For its treatment of all the questions involving faith and aesthetics, Ryken's work is invaluable.

Considering the Source
What motivates the creative person? The artist is impelled by motives other than the desire for money. There is something more important in the balance. As John Gardner has expressed it, "True art is *by its nature moral*. . . . As a chemist's experiment tests the laws of nature and dramatically reveals the truth or falsity of scientific hypotheses, moral art tests values and rouses trustworthy feelings about the better and the worse in human action."[2] (Gardner was referring specifically to narrative art, a category that encompasses most movies.)

If the role of art is thus morally serious, then the true artist will be at great pains to deal with a subject in just the right way. It would hardly be consistent to handle one's subject any old way if it really matters. (Mr. Gardner would add that it would not even be *moral*.) Therefore the artist accepts the responsibility of becoming master of his or her medium. And this means exploring all the expressive potential that the medium offers.

When the artist takes on such a moral burden and accepts this challenge in his craft, it deserves a response in us, the audience. Our task is to equip ourselves to receive what the creative person offers us. With regard to film, there is more to this than we usually acknowledge. The first requirement is a willingness to give our attention to serious works. This is half the battle in today's environment, where purely commercial films monopolize public attention. When we choose to seek out the work of a serious artist, we do the artist and ourselves a service. We can then give our attention to his methods and the language he communicates in.

While doing research for this book, I enjoyed exploring a variety of works on the craft of film. I would urge any Christian who wants to appreciate and enjoy movies more to read Arthur Knight's *The Liveliest Art* and James Monaco's *How to Read a Film*. There are many more, but I especially recommend these two as starting points.

Mr. Monaco, in an early chapter titled "Film as Art," demonstrates how movies possess the qualities of nearly all the other arts. The links with painting and still photography hardly need to be pointed out, nor does the connection with live drama. The narrative function shared with the novel is essential. There are affinities with music in elements such as rhythm and harmony (these exist quite apart from the use of music as background). However, while film is clearly allied to these older arts, it has its own peculiar dynamics, its own laws. It speaks to us in ways that only film can.

The Language of Film

Almost all movies are rendered in the same basic language, with an inexhaustible visual vocabulary and well-developed grammar and syntax. These allow directors and their editors to connect pieces of visual information so that they flow as effective narrative. Those directors who can fashion a coherent, affecting experience with this material (e.g., Hitchcock, Lean, Levinson) have a style, just as those writers do who fashion a graceful or powerful flow of words (Austen, Hemmingway, Faulkner).

One way to estimate the nature and scope of the movies' language is to stop and consider what it grew out of. There was a time, at the beginning of the century, when movies were made with hardly any form or technique at all. There wasn't even a story—just a scene or vignette, such as a flirtation in the park or the arrival of a train. The action was decided upon (and *maybe* written down), the playing area selected, and the camera started. When the skit was completed or when the film ran out, the movie was done. There was no shift in time or space, no variation in viewpoint or distance from the action. What happened in front of the camera was the movie.

Consider the road that had to be travelled in order for film to get where it is today. The very idea that a movie could contain a number of different scenes, the creation of a method to link these scenes together, the discovery that each individual moment could be rendered in countless ways by the camera—these are all steps in the development of motion picture art, and they were taken by creative pioneers such as Porter, Griffith, and Eisenstein. But these contributions are only a fraction of the film heritage. The enormous growth in sophistication of sets, the introduction and refinement of sound, and especially the evolution of lighting (so often taken for granted) required decades of labor and inspiration.

Most of these developments have been signalized by the appearance of classic works: *Birth of a Nation, Battleship Potemkin, Citizen Kane, Open City.* Why do we remain unaware of the craft of film and the particular accomplishments that resulted in such classics? Parents exert themselves heroically to have children read and appreciate literary classics. We insist that young people have at least a passing acquaintance with Shakespeare, Dickens, and Mark Twain. But we accept complete ignorance of Griffith, Eisenstein, Jean Renoir, and John Ford.

This must relate to the view of film as light entertainment. A movie (if we are to like it) should offer nothing upsetting, nothing that would demand any real exercise of the mind, and at all costs, nothing that could change our outlook on the world. Give us a little fear that is relieved in the end; give us suspense that is momentarily heightened and then released; give us simplistic romance; give us the satisfaction of revenge for terrible wrongs. And for those of us who are religious, give us that phenomenon called "uplift," by which we leave the theater strongly assured of the power of good to overcome evil, and of our own identification with the good!

Now the artist—when he or she possesses a mature outlook—knows that human goodness can be scarce and indistinct, that human love may not conquer all, that there is never much sweetness in revenge. And the artist has the audacity to want to show us the truth in regard to goodness and love and justice. No wonder this challenges us, or that we want to shrink from it. But here again, the easy way is the way of least reward for the Christian.

The Unexpected Artist

Why was Jesus a storyteller? Why did he not just go about explaining everything in plain words, with a straightforward presentation of what we should believe and how we should act? This is not a frivolous question, because it points us rather clearly to the uses of art. Understanding human nature as he did, Jesus was well aware of the way our fears and our selfishness make us impervious to certain influences. We build walls in our minds to guard us from troubling questions. Jesus knew that the best way to penetrate these barriers of self-interest, to dig under these walls, was to couch the truth in terms of a fictional narrative.

When we receive the words "There was a man who had two sons," or "The kingdom of heaven is like a king who wanted to settle accounts with his servants," it is an invitation. Such opening lines stimulate definite responses, but not anxiety or insecurity. They provoke curiosity, sympathy, even humor. But once we have been taken into the fictional realm, we cannot help following all the way to the conclusion. Whatever will become of the prodigal? How will the king deal with his servants? When the conclusion is reached, the point is driven home. We cannot escape, except by the mightiest efforts of avoidance and self-deception, because the process of identification in this kind of experience makes us ask, What if it had been me?

This was only one part of Jesus' message and ministry, but it was a vital part. With the parables he was continually getting past the defenses and the disinterest of his hearers. He still does, even today.

This process is illustrated more dramatically in the Old Testament. The career of David, as related in the books of Samuel, is absorbing from start to finish. No episode is more gripping than that of David's "great sin"—his adultery with Bathsheba and the elimination of her husband. Quite beyond this sex and violence, the dramatic focal point is God's calling David to account through the agency of Nathan the prophet.

What happened is worth a close review, because Nathan's method of dealing with David was to give him a brief fiction narrative. He resorted to art. "There were two men in a certain town, one rich and the other poor," he began. And the royal audience was hooked. As David listened, the prophet related in detail how the poor man loved a little ewe lamb, which was his only possession. "It was like a daughter to him," said Nathan, and he continued,

> *"Now a traveler came to the rich man, but the rich man refrained from taking one of his own sheep or cattle to prepare a meal for the traveler who had come to him. Instead, he took the ewe lamb that belonged to the poor man and prepared it for the one who had come to him."*
>
> *David burned with anger against the man and said to Nathan, "As surely as the LORD lives, the man who did this deserves to die! He must pay for that lamb four times over, because he did such a thing and had no pity."*
>
> *Then Nathan said to David, "You are the man!"*
>
> 2 Samuel 12:4-7

David was stunned. His conviction was complete. He was forced to look at the truth about himself. The episode illustrates the unique value of the storytelling art. If Nathan had not caused David first to identify with the imaginary victim in his story, he might not have succeeded in his mission. If he had walked in and made a direct accusation of the king, David would have had him thrown out at once.

Identification, Please

Nathan's art had its effect by evoking sympathy with the subject of the story. This happens to be one of the things that movies do best. Even the most routine acting and camera work can have us seeing things from the hero's point of view in an instant. Once this is established, we are able to experience what the character experiences and learn from this directly.

Let us take an example from the work of a legendary star. Bette Davis made a career of playing unusual, often unsympathetic characters. It has been said that her triumph—perhaps her genius—lies in the fact that she made each of these roles compelling; we care about the character whether or not we admire her. One of Davis's best-known features is *Now, Voyager*, in which her character is the victim of a tyrannical mother. The movie was immensely popular, and Davis received a heavy volume of mail from women who identified with the situation. Ms. Davis has said, "You *can't imagine* the women who wrote to me after that film saying, 'I realize what I did to my children.' "[3]

The movies are a popular art, and the familiar process of identification—of claiming a character to live inside and root for—provides the greatest pleasure for most audiences. However, there have always been film artists who use audience identification to gain more complex results than rooting for the fellow in the white hat or cringing for the threatened heroine.

It is these artists who have given us some of the most worthwhile film achievements from the Christian point of view. They have set themselves the difficult and risky goal of leading us to identify with people radically different from us. These characters may have become alien or disreputable because of error or circumstance, or they may have been stricken with blighting handicaps. In any case, they are the sort of humans that we habitually consider *other than* ourselves. A distinguished line of movies runs from early works probing the effects of vice to modern films that deal with physically and emotionally scarred persons.

In 1932, *I am a Fugitive from a Chain Gang* was one of the first attempts to examine the social problems of our nation. (It led to reform of the penal system in Georgia, where the incidents that inspired the story occurred.) *The Informer* of 1935 remains one of John Ford's most honored films; it caused audiences to relate to a flawed, desperate human being in the alien setting of Irish rebellion. It is probably the first American film whose protagonist is not an admirable person.

Ford's *The Grapes of Wrath*, released in 1940, draws us into the suffering of the poor during the Great Depression. With supreme artistry (especially in the camera work of Gregg Toland), it deals with the unpleasant facts regarding dispossessed farmers in Oklahoma and exploited laborers in California. We cannot deny this historical truth, even though we may recognize that the characters and dialogue have been sentimentalized by their creators. *The Grapes of Wrath* demonstrates a link between significant content and inspired treatment that typifies the most cherished works in all the arts.

Since the middle of the century, films dealing with social injustice have become fairly common (*Gentleman's Agreement, Twelve Angry Men, Edge of the City, Bad Day at Black Rock*, etc., down to *Mississippi Burning*).

Regrettably, they have often run to clichés. In the last decade or so, filmmakers have achieved more—especially from an artistic standpoint—when they have concentrated on particular individuals struggling with an unfair fate. David Lynch's *The Elephant Man* (1980) might be termed an extreme example of this kind of film. Lynch's treatment of a bizarre and potentially repelling subject is in the end a heart-warming and inspiring experience. An ambitious essay in the art of film, it succeeds in showing us a great deal about selfishness and fear, but more about love and courage.

A similarly challenging subject was handled with even greater success in *My Left Foot* (1989). Like *Elephant Man*, this is based on a true story; it has the further advantage of following the autobiography of a gifted writer. The task is forbidding—how can we be made to identify with a character who appears to have no control of limbs, no capacity for communication or even rational thought? But again the director triumphed, with the help of a remarkable performance by Daniel Day Lewis. The result is an incomparable excursion in awareness, and in the appreciation of life's possibilities.

Such films as these achieve their impact by making us identify with the unlovely, the forsaken, and the hopeless. They are like moral binoculars, bringing us into close touch with subjects and persons that we naturally and habitually avoid. Binoculars, of course, will show fine detail; in these cases the moral detail might include intense bitterness and harsh language. But the subjects of these films are the kind of people— along with all who are victimized and forsaken—that we are called to concern ourselves with as Christians.

Thank goodness for artists who have the skill and the commitment to make this easier for us! If we neglect the assistance they offer, we do so at the peril of our own moral condition. Yet how often do we hear or make the protest that this kind of film is "too dreary" or "too depressing" for us to watch?

While many great films help us to identify with those unlike ourselves, some directors take up a different and more subtle challenge. They explore the moral predicament of individuals who *are* like us, illuminating the inner nature of respectable, successful people. One such director is Woody Allen, whose work merits our attention even while his personal life occasions dismay and disappointment. Whatever judgment we make of him, it is clear that Allen is among the most serious-minded of all contemporary artists.

In films such as *Hannah and Her Sisters* (1986) and *Crimes and Misdemeanors* (1989) Allen offers a painstaking moral scrutiny of characters who are intelligent, successful, and in many ways appealing. The earlier film focuses on one man's infidelity to his loving, near-perfect wife. Michael Caine and Barbara Hershey (as his sister-in-law!) portray the adulterous pair with vivid poignancy. They learn a bitter lesson, and in this respect the movie is an update of an old-fashioned morality tale.

Crimes and Misdemeanors is Allen's most serious attempt to deal with profound moral and theological issues. Early comedies like *Love and Death* or *Annie Hall* danced flippantly about the great questions: Does God exist? Do personal choices have meaning? This movie addresses them in dead earnest. Here again Allen dissects the moral experience of respected individuals who still reveal our basic sinfulness. The film asks us to identify with a man who finds himself in an adulterous relationship and descends gradually, one might say routinely, to an even more monstrous guilt. A movie like this leads us to examine our own readiness to deceive ourselves about the price of getting what we want. And again, it does so by forcing us to identify with problematic characters.

A Sin of Not Knowing

In his illuminating study *Whatever Became of Sin?* the late Dr. Karl Menninger discussed a modern tendency to avoid the truth about the needs of the world around us. He claimed that "there is a sin of not doing, of not knowing, of not finding out what we must do" that we cannot tolerate if we care about our own spiritual condition.[4] It doesn't matter that we may be in the majority with our habits of ignorance. "Call it sloth . . . laziness, callousness or whatever—if refusal to learn permits the continuance of destructive evil, such willful ignorance is surely wrong."[5]

Christians do not need to be told this by a noted psychologist. He was only reiterating what is implicit in the entire ministry of our Savior. (For a quick refresher, consult the parable of the Good Samaritan in Luke 10.) Moreover, the principle turns up long before the New Testament period. In the book of the prophet Hosea we read these terrible words:

You stumble day and night,
and the prophets stumble with you. . . .
My people are destroyed from
  lack of knowledge.
Because you have rejected knowledge,
I also reject you as my priests;
because you have ignored the law of
  your God,
I also will ignore your children.
Hosea 4:5-6

The Christian who would follow the law of the Lord as Jesus inter-preted it to us must beware of the sin of ignorance. We cannot begin to love a neighbor if we refuse to acknowledge who he or she is. Our "love" can have no consequence if we reject an understanding of the neighbor's situation. Jesus is the ultimate model of this principle. But through the centuries artists have been engaged in helping us make the connection to our fellow man in his needs. Too often we have not troubled ourselves to pay attention.

Even artists who seem alien or hostile to our tradition can sometimes merit careful regard. This is the case with a filmmaker like Ingmar Bergman (to name one example), who has proven both his genius and his seriousness. In *Fanny and Alexander,* one of Bergman's more widely known films, the two children are tyrannized by a stepfather who is a minister in the Swedish church. But the effect is light years away from the caricature process of films like *Carrie* and *Footloose.* In these, the "Chris-tian" parents are formula ogres made to order for the youth market. Bergman's portrait of a threatening pastor/father is based on recollec-tions of his own father, who was a minister and a severe ruler of his household.

These segments of *Fanny and Alexander* do not provide comfortable viewing for Christians. Nevertheless, those who are willing to look will find Bergman's work a powerful resource. It can help us evaluate our own relations with children and the living of our testimony before them.

The pastor father in *Babette's Feast* offers a fine comparison to Bergman's portrait. In this wonderful Danish film, the father's strict piety is complemented by gentleness and humility. The effect of his personality on those around him is radically different.

Unfortunately, these films and others like them remain unknown in many church communities. And it isn't always just a lack of awareness. Some Christians purposely dismiss the work of any artist not recognized as a believer. They assume that those who are not orthodox Christians have nothing worthwhile to say. No attempt is made to judge the artist by his fruits. How easily this plays in with our natural laziness; how inconsistent it is with biblical teaching!

When I notice persistent pain in a tooth, or when my car breaks down, I don't ask if the dentist or the garage mechanic is a believer. I accept their expertise on its own terms, because what I need is someone who will do good work. To a certain extent, the same should hold true for my emotional and intellectual needs. Our God is the God of truth. Whoever helps me to see the truth about myself or the world I live in is a resource God has provided.

This is not a simple proposition, and not an easy one to uphold with respect to popular arts. It requires diligence and a careful exercise of judgment. There are writers and filmmakers uncounted who deal in lies, deceptions, or half-truths. But, by the grace of God, I am not helpless to discern which voices are false. And my awareness of them cannot become an excuse to ignore the conscientious truth-tellers in the world of secular culture. I may ignore them, and my church may ignore them, at the greatest peril.

One of my favorite Old Testament passages has always been the story of Balaam's Ass (as we *used* to call the animal). I could never hear this episode without finding an unmistakable hint of comedy—maybe because the character of Balaam is so cantankerous he seems to cry out for portrayal by a great character actor like Charles Laughton. The trouble was that Balaam, though nominally the servant of the Lord, was blind to what lay directly in his path, threatening destruction. But God allowed the not-so-dumb animal to see and to respond. Finally Balaam's eyes were opened:

> The angel of the LORD asked him, "Why have you beaten your donkey these three times? I have come here to oppose you because your path is a reckless one before me. The donkey saw me and turned away from me these three times. If

she had not turned away, I would certainly have killed you by now, but I would have spared her."
Numbers 22:32-33

How many artists there must be who can feel a rueful sympathy with this poor animal—able to see clearly, able to warn, but vilified and steadfastly ignored by the servants of God who are bent upon their own course.

One of the most distinguished film writers of our time is also a highly successful dramatist. Robert Bolt was responsible for the scripts of such impressive features as *The Mission* and *Lawrence of Arabia*. He wrote the play *A Man for All Seasons* and the film adaptation, which won the Academy award in 1966 for Best Picture.

Bolt is the premier example of a non-Christian writer who is at the same time a serious, morally responsible artist. In discussing his approach to *A Man for All Seasons*, he stated plainly, "I am not a Catholic nor even in the meaningful sense of the word a Christian."[6] Nevertheless, the work is one of the most inspiring representations of faith and courage that has ever reached the stage. The artist could not be true to his subject and have it come out any other way.

Not all artists are guided by moral concerns as Bolt is, nor is it common for them to focus on men of faith like More, or the doomed missionaries in *The Mission*. Most moviemakers are decidedly more secular in outlook. They are not necessarily less important to the concerned Christian. If we diligently seek out the serious moral artist among the cynics and impostors, we will be rewarded in ample measure.

Higher Goals, Higher Risks
One thing that distinguishes the true artist is a willingness to take risks. Unfortunately, this is why some of us avoid the artist and his achievement; we don't want risk, we want repetition. But the very concept of creativity requires a venturing into the undiscovered and the unfamiliar.

If a filmmaker has anything to say, he or she must sometimes risk being misunderstood. When we acknowledge this, we can recognize an important corollary for viewers: those who know the language are less likely to miss the meaning of a film as it is conceived by its maker. The audience that brings greater seriousness to a picture will derive more insight from it, but seriousness needs to be supplemented with knowledge. As James Monaco reminds us, "People who are highly experienced in film, highly literate visually . . . see more and hear more than people who seldom go to movies. An education in the quasi-language of film opens up greater potential meaning for the observer."[7]

While greater film literacy will help us to benefit from good movies, it can also enable us to find profit in certain films that are not outstanding, or not successful in the conventional sense. Some categories of failure have little or no bearing on how we relate to a film as Christians.

Chariots of Fire, for example, was dismissed by a number of critics. Some found that its script lacked coherence because it dealt with two protagonists who had nothing to do with each other. Some called the story uninteresting because it was simply about people winning races. The first criticism is valid. The latter is incomprehensible to me, since the story offers the drama of Christian values in conflict with the pressures of worldly success.

Likewise, certain critics found *The Mission* to be pompous and lacking in coherence. I agree that Robert Bolt's screenplay is not a model of symmetry, as I also agree with those who felt that Robert De Niro was miscast in such a film. But these are mere quibbles compared with the importance of the goals of the film, and the truths it so painfully sets forth.

Sometimes a movie requires our indulgence because it tries a bit too hard to be significant. Brian De Palma's *Casualties of War,* based on a tragic incident in Vietnam, was scorned by critics for its earnestness. Unfortunately, the first scene of the film suggests that De Palma was not born to direct war movies; his choices make the action seem unlikely if not ludicrous. But from this point on the story increases in believability and power. The movie becomes a profound study of Christian morality in the crucible of modern war.

Achieving greater sophistication as viewers can make us more tolerant of flaws in an ambitious work. It can also free us from the popular prejudice against out-of-the-ordinary methods. This point becomes crucial as the mass audience is more and more conditioned in its taste by television.

TV has affected audience expectations in two important and interrelated areas. One is the phenomenon of the short attention span; the other is the rapid-fire style of editing that both exploits and reinforces it. The problem of the short attention span is well known by now, especially among educators. Television viewers are raised on a diet of story development in eight-minute chunks. After each chunk comes a one-and-a-half minute interval of complete mental disengagement induced by commercials. With this pattern of training, no wonder some people have difficulty following a serious full-length motion picture.

The effects of television's editing style and tempo are less obvious. TV trains us to expect a lightning-fast exposition of story or theme with quick cuts from one image to the next. Deriving from the "art" of the commercial, but increasingly evident in regular programming, this approach works well for certain limited purposes: it grabs attention; it builds a momentary sense of excitement. But its ideal function is still selling. Such a style gets the audience to feel without thinking—thought would be counter to the aims of the sponsor. It is useless for an artistic purpose such as character development.

The up-tempo style of television has had great influence on movie production. More and more movies display the speed and superficiality of TV ads. The corollary development within the audience is predictable: Those who possess only a TV level of literacy are put off by a slower pace. They can't wait for something else to happen on the screen. As a result they are unable to appreciate films that take their time in developing complex ideas or revealing rich, multifaceted characters.

Viewers thus limited will never be able to benefit from many great European films, nor from the work of such English and American masters as John Ford, David Lean, Stanley Kubrick, Robert Altman, and Barry Levinson. Slow does not always equal good, of course, but when we can't respond to anything but television pacing, we will never know when it does. Christians don't need this handicap in laying hold of all that our movie heritage offers us.

An increased awareness of the art of film will not save our souls. Learning to relish the deep-focus camera work of *Citizen Kane* or the famous tracking shots of Alfred Hitchcock will not make us better

Christians. But gaining the ability to savor film art will add much to our leisure lives, and perhaps help to keep us from drowning in secular culture.

Love's Labor Gained

We have not yet touched on one element of art that may be the most important. It will never be discussed in classes on art theory, film history, or any other subject. It is the element of love.

Love is the unseen force that has influenced almost every great artistic endeavor through the centuries. The love that emanates from the creator—or does not—determines the quality and nature of the work. It is a principle as old as ancient Greece, where the sculptor Pygmalion was said to have cherished the woman he himself had carved from ivory. It can be discerned in the work of painters, as in the compassion of a Rembrandt or a van Gogh. It can be sensed in literature, especially in the English tradition from Shakespeare through Dickens, and on to modern writers as diverse as J. D. Salinger and Alan Paton.

It is not found in every great artist, but it is in many, and it is in those who have something to say to the Christian. As John Gardner puts it,

> In art, morality and love are inextricably bound: we affirm what is good—for the characters in particular and for humanity in general—because we care. The artist who has no strong feelings about his characters—the artist who can feel compassionate only about his words or ideas—has no urgent reason to think hard about the characters' problems, the "themes" in his fiction.[8]

Gardner goes on to assert that "without compassion—without real and deep love for his 'subjects' (the people he writes about and, by extension, all human beings)—no artist can summon the will to make true art."[9]

We are fortunate that our movie heritage offers so many good examples of what Gardner is talking about. The quality of love or compassion is unmistakable in recent works like *Stand and Deliver*, *Driving Miss Daisy*, and even Disney's magnificent *Beauty and the Beast*. It is the quality that saves a film like *Fried Green Tomatoes* from its own sentimental contrivances (with the help of some brilliant acting). And now, by means of the VCR, we can explore this quality in the work of film artists from Griffith to the present. Among those who have most to offer are Frank Capra, Preston Sturges, Sir Richard Attenborough, Robert Benton, Bruce Beresford, and Bill Forsyth.

Of all these directors, Frank Capra was the most unabashed in talking about love. Commenting on his goals for the film *You Can't Take it With You,* he spoke of "something deeper, something greater" than mere comedy entertainment. The play he was filming offered the opportunity to dramatize the Golden Rule: "What the world's churches were preaching . . . my universal language of film might say more entertainingly to movie audiences, *if*—it could prove, in theatrical conflict, that Christ's spiritual law can be the most powerful sustaining force in anyone's life."[10]

Frank Capra may not have been a great artist. He was not a profound religious thinker, and may not have been a Christian in any conventional sense. He was a great entertainer who happened to be refreshingly sincere in his love for humanity. Many of his films—especially the pure comedies—are laughing at just the right things in the unregenerate nature of man. And in all of them, love is maintained as a powerful redeeming force. When we watch *You Can't Take it With You* (Academy Awards for Best Film and Best Director, 1938) we cannot miss what Capra wanted to communicate.

Many other artists express their love for mankind by creatively, urgently drawing our attention to the errors that drag us down and separate us from God. This function of art is prophetic—not in the sense of foretelling events, but in pushing the audience to confront the truth. But the most effective art is not that which indulges in fingerpointing, but that which woos us to partake of the love that is felt by the Creator. The numerous biblical scenes of Rembrandt are designed to evoke the very spirit of compassion that fills the New Testament. We have already observed the success of Dickens in moving his readers to compassion and an active concern for the unfortunate. Vincent van Gogh, one of the heirs of Rembrandt, painted picture after picture that conveys an unmistakable burden of concern for the suffering of his subjects. The serious moviemaker is often in this noble tradition.

Some artists are born to decorate our existence with beauty, the way the bluebird does. We need this, of course, but we need other artists just as much: the truth-tellers, the illuminators. Van Gogh gave us sunflowers and irises to ravish the eye and gladden the heart, but he also gave us unforgettable impressions of starving, broken humanity. In the latter we find—*if we are paying attention*—an invitation to suffer and care for our fellow beings in something like the way the artist did.

Unlimited Opportunities

The movies may have produced no van Gogh, no Rembrandt. They may not have produced a Dickens or a Victor Hugo. But they have come close—and sadly, most of us don't realize it.

The coming of the VCR should spur Christians to reach beyond our customary negligence. We now have the opportunity to fit ourselves for more intelligent choices in entertainment. We have a second chance to receive the prophetic offering of the screen artist, instead of floating on the lazy stream of cinematic best-sellers.

Now we can always experience the sugar-coated silliness of *Field of Dreams*, but we can also see *The Trip to Bountiful* or *I Never Sang for My Father*, and have our eyes opened to deeper and more complex realities in the parent-child relationship. We can enjoy a star vehicle like *Dead Poets Society* and bask in the glow of its romanticized hero; we can also experience films that treat education and coming of age with more compelling honesty, films like *Stand and Deliver* or *Educating Rita*.

We can swallow the can't-miss combination of sentimentality and eroticism found in *Ghost*. We can also witness a masterpiece of heartbreaking intensity like *The Dead*. (In a lighter vein, we can savor the entertaining *Heaven Can Wait* of 1978, which is far more serious and more intelligent than *Ghost*.)

The subject of war has inspired some of the greatest movies and some of the worst. Those who find the war film appealing can now reacquaint themselves with the masterpieces of the genre. A number of these are impressive because they present the physical experience so effectively— the masses of men and materiel in frantic or inexorable movement (*Patton, Tora! Tora! Tora!, A Bridge Too Far*, etc.). But a second category deserves the attention of Christians even more than these. Certain directors place the experience of war in a deeply considered moral context. They recognize that the very extremities of combat, where men and women face the risk of instant death, lay bare the essential qualities of the soul. The meaning of life can be weighed most carefully when its possession is most uncertain. These directors have left a priceless legacy in films such as *All Quiet on the Western Front, Grand Illusion, Gallipoli, Das Boot (The Boat), The Highest Honor,* and *Glory.*

One area that doesn't fit a genre label, but cannot be ignored, is the body of films based on classic novels. The great novels have attracted movie directors and producers from the beginning of the industry. In some cases a good novel has been the basis for an even greater film. The difficulties of translating the novel to film—and there are many—are examined fully in Joy Gould Boyum's book *Double Exposure: Fiction Into Film.* Fortunately the successes are too numerous to list, but they run from William Wyler's *Dodsworth* (1936) to Christine Edzard's delightful *Little Dorrit* (1988) and the Merchant-Ivory films *A Room with a View* (1988) and *Howard's End* (1992).

Raymond Chandler was a master of detective fiction whose novels inspired numerous films. (Howard Hawks's *The Big Sleep*, with Bogart and Bacall, is the best known.) Chandler was more than a great entertainer; he was also an accomplished literary artist. Once in an essay on mystery writing he observed that "In everything that can be called art there is a quality of redemption."[11] There may be more to this than even Chandler suspected. Some art appears to lack such a quality altogether, but there is more that clearly justifies his claim. Our movie heritage is rich in this redemptive element. But in order to recognize it, we have to be looking for it.

We can be glad for the opportunities that movies give us to escape, to feel good, even to think well of ourselves. But as Christians we have to recognize our need for the kind of art that helps us comprehend the way things really are, the way *we* really are—not just the way we wish we were. For we are hardly different from those self-satisfied spectators who squinted at the young rabbi from Galilee, listening in spite of themselves as he told them a story; hardly different from the Old Testament king who was kidding himself about sin and guilt and responsibility. We need to let the storyteller come into the room who can grab us by the imagination and say, "Thou art the man!"

Notes to Chapter 10

1. Quoted in Peter Bogdanovich, *John Ford*, Studio Vista Series (London: Movie Magazine Limited, 1967), 108.

2. John Gardner, *On Moral Fiction* (New York: Basic Books, 1978), 19.

3. Quoted in Judith Crist, *Take 22: Moviemakers on Moviemaking* (New York: Viking Penguin, 1984), 272.

4. Karl Menninger, M. D., *Whatever Became of Sin?* (New York: Hawthorn Books, 1973), 148.

5. Menninger, 147.

6. Robert Bolt, Preface to *A Man for All Seasons*, (New York: Vintage Books, a Division of Random House, 1962), xii.

7. James Monaco, *How to Read a Film* (New York: Oxford University Press, 1981), 121.

8. Gardner, 84.

9. Gardner, 85.

10. Frank Capra, *The Name Above the Title* (New York: Vintage Books, a division of Random House, 1985), 241.

11. Raymond Chandler, *The Simple Art of Murder* (New York: Vintage Books, a division of Random House, 1988), 18. First published in 1950.

Chapter 11

Habits of
Appreciation

*And this is my prayer: that your love may abound more and more in knowledge
and depth of insight, so that you may be able to discern what is best and may be
pure and blameless until the day of Christ.*
Philippians 1:9-10

Do movies matter?

This is the key question when we look for a satisfying approach to
screen entertainment. Many believers share the popular notion that
movies are a simple diversion, without significance. The idea is appealing
because it is so comfortable. It allows us to ignore any challenging insight
a movie may contain.

The fundamental premise of this book is that movies do matter. Movies
are an important part of our culture, and for many reasons they deserve
to be taken seriously by today's Christians. The viewing of a film always
has the potential to enrich or enlighten even while it gives us pleasure.
But whether it will actually do these things depends largely on us.

There are definite steps we can take to make our experience of a movie
significant. We exercise control over the event in two important ways.
First, we decide on the content simply by choosing one film to watch
instead of another. Second, we make a number of choices regarding the
conditions in which the film is viewed. Unfortunately, our choices in both
of these areas can be made carelessly; we pick movies at random and view
them in a setting and a manner we have adopted with no thought at all.
This chapter is devoted to practical suggestions about these decisions. It

will deal with good habits in movie-watching, habits that work for our full appreciation of what a movie has to offer.

Much of our discussion thus far has involved the question of what is worth watching on film. We have touched on various strategies for picking out the good and avoiding the worthless. One of these (mentioned in chapter 5) involved alertness to information provided by the press. At this point we again turn our attention to those much-maligned experts, the movie critics.

The Critics—Who Needs Them?

Whenever I hear people discussing a movie and saying whether they enjoyed it or not, I am likely to hear the question "Did you see what that reviewer in the paper said about it?" The comments that usually follow are not made in tones of warm admiration. Indeed, for as long as I have been aware of reviews and critics, I have listened to complaints about their meanness and stupidity. I have sometimes added to the chorus myself.

If you read the work of one or two reviewers in a local newspaper each week, it is easy to get the impression they are all ill-humored cynics. Many of them seem to take a particular delight in attacking the most popular movies. The writers in turn become a popular object of scorn; some people even say they plan their moviegoing by selecting whatever film the critic does not like. This is the extreme of the "who needs them?" attitude.

But the truth is that we need them if our movie-going and video-watching are to be rewarding. The critic or reviewer is one of our resources in developing good habits of awareness and appreciation. Most of us are able to consult not one but several reviewers in evaluating a given film. However, the more we read or listen to any one critic, the more we are in a position to benefit from that critic's observations.

Some people draw a contrast between movie *reviewers* and true critics. It is a useful distinction: The reviewer serves to familiarize us with a film in regard to its content and its personnel; the critic takes us deeper into the meaning of the film and its range of success and failures. It has been said that we should consult the reviewer before we see a film, and read the critic to understand and appreciate films we have already seen.

Both the reviewer and the more serious critic are valuable, and they don't have to be geniuses to be worth reading. We may form an initial attitude to a film based on what a newspaper reviewer writes—and what we know about the outlook of that writer. Fortunately, we can always find more than one reviewer to consult, and thus we can compare reactions (they often vary widely).

Comparing reviews is a good idea because the service the typical reviewer offers is limited. Reviewers, whether they appear in the daily newspaper, in *Time* or *Newsweek,* or on TV, always work within narrow constraints of space or air-time. Often they are under pressure to crank out a piece overnight after a movie has opened. (As mundane as it seems, this is an important difference between a movie review and real movie criticism. The critic does not limit herself or himself to a thumbnail, a capsule, or a few paragraphs of print.) The average review answers only routine questions about a film. If a comedy, does it make me laugh? If a drama, does it sustain involvement? Is the plot believable? And so on.

These routine judgments based on a first impression are important to me because they may be the only information I have before deciding on the movie. Thus the more familiar I am with the person making the judgments, the more accurately I can assess them. If the reviewer always praises slam-bang action movies, I will remember this when he passes judgment on *The Whales of August* or *Sarah, Plain and Tall.* If he invariably registers enthusiasm over "steamy" performances and directors that "break new ground" with sexual themes, I may discount his praise of *Body Heat* or *Basic Instinct.*

All of us have our biases, including reviewers. The more alert we are to this, the better use we can make of a reviewer's comments. If the reviewer proves to be genuinely objective (perhaps by *acknowledging* his or her bias), we can treasure the commentary even more.

Reviewers serve what is basically a publicity function (unlike true critics). Even so, they are invaluable for telling us what is out there. Theater ads are not reliable. Often the films with the least intrinsic merit get the biggest, flashiest advertisements. The best pictures may only get postage-stamp notices in the Friday entertainment section. But a good reviewer will be alert to the arrival of an unheralded masterpiece. If we are in the habit of following the reviewer's column, we may be tipped off to a wonderful film that could be missed completely in the ads.

There are those who claim to avoid reviewers and criticism because they don't want to be affected by the opinion of another person. Theoretically there is some merit in this, but our likes and dislikes are usually influenced by outside forces whether we know it or not. Some people make a fine show of independence when it comes to reviews, but end up choosing a movie on the basis of what their best friend's cousin said about it. We must never be in awe of the reviewer's opinion (the good reviewers certainly don't want it this way), but we cheat ourselves by refusing to make the most of their knowledge and acumen.

Because the critic makes a practice of noticing flaws and inconsistencies in films, we need not assume that he wants to find them, or that he wishes failure on the filmmaker. It is simply that the critic begins—as most of us do not—with a detailed knowledge of what it takes to make an excellent film. The critic is alive to all of the possibilities, as we are not. And when the critic takes note of certain shortcomings, it does not mean that he is rejecting the movie as a whole.

The most valuable thing we can learn from the movie critic may be how to evaluate a film justly by taking into account all of its strengths *and* weaknesses. Too often the thoughtless or immature moviegoer prefers a blunt thumbs-up or thumbs-down reaction. If he had a good time at the movie, he will say it was a "great flick," and he won't listen to questions about inconsistency of plot or contradictory signals in regard to values. By the same token, if he did not happen to enjoy the movie, then the movie was no good. "Don't waste your time!" is the verdict. (He would never admit that his inability to appreciate a movie was not the movie's fault.)

It is true that there are some one-sided, immature reviewers. But they rarely last long or rise to positions where they reach a wide audience. And there are always other and better critics to consult.

As a model of a thorough and balanced review, I recall the piece that veteran Pauline Kael wrote on the movie *Glory*. This was a stirring Civil War film that told the story of America's first black army regiment. Unlike the few inches in my local newspaper, Ms. Kael's review covered nearly two and a half magazine pages. She began, not with press-agent hype, but with a look at the real historical setting of the story. This took up an introductory paragraph of some two hundred words. Moving on to the movie's treatment of the subject, she found much to admire and much that was less satisfying. She evaluated the performers in regard to the different demands of their roles, pointing out, for example, the wide difference between the acting styles of Denzel Washington and Morgan Freeman (each is effective in its place). She gave attention to certain effects that the director achieved and some that he might have achieved but didn't. She implied that some of his shortcomings derived from inexperience. She summed up her impressions in the following sentence: " 'Glory' isn't a great film, but it's a good film on a great subject."[1]

This kind of review is accurate, generous, and just. It takes enough space—goes into enough detail—to be all those things. I went to see *Glory*. I admired some of the things Kael had singled out for praise. I noticed some of the weaknesses she had also pointed out. And I loved the movie.

One thing that puts some people off from the work of movie critics is fear—fear of not being able to understand what they are talking about, fear of being made to feel dumb. I have experienced these feelings myself. But while we are all likely to end up in water over our heads occasionally, it is a mistake to be shy about what the experts say of a film. We never have to agree. We don't always have to understand. But if we keep reading we may *come* to understand; if we back off and avoid reading we never will.

One concept that seems to intimidate moviegoers more than any other is symbolism. A certain dread of symbolism—or anxiety about not catching on—keeps people away from some movies, especially foreign ones. It also makes them reluctant to read the critics. But the wisest critics and the greatest directors recognize that symbolism has only a limited role if it is to be valuable. Some directors handle it playfully, not always knowing or caring what a given symbol means. The true artist knows that the most effective symbols act on our minds and emotions without even being noticed. As with all artistic devices, the best do not call attention to themselves.

The well-known critic Judith Crist has a good story about symbolism. At a time when she was reviewing for the New York *Herald Tribune* and Bosley Crowther was the critic for the *Times*, they happened to discuss a new film by Alain Resnais (one of France's New Wave directors of the 50s). Crowther admitted to Crist that he could not understand the symbolism of a white horse that appeared in the film. Crist relates the rest of the horse story as follows:

> I was deeply depressed: I hadn't even thought it was a symbol. A short time later I asked Resnais; the white horse, it turned out, was the only one available at the stable for that day's shooting.[2]

Reliable film commentators will always be helpful—not pretentious or confusing—in regard to the more complicated aspects of film. Besides helping us to understand a particular movie, they are an important source of information about film history and the wider cultural background of a production. They can relate the film to others on a similar theme. They can enlighten us about earlier versions of the same story. The best reviewers (Ms. Kael up until her retirement in 1990 was an excellent example) have done their homework on all of the relevant background.

If the film is a treatment of a novel like *The Color Purple* or *The Age of Innocence*, the good critic will have read and understood the novel. If it is based on actual events such as *Reversal of Fortune* or *JFK*, the critic will have done the required homework on the events themselves. Thus he can offer insights about the way a film relates to contemporary trends, or the way it exploits popular anxieties. The best critics are intelligent observers, not only of films, but of society as a whole.

Doing Our Own Digging

The advantages to be gained from reading a good critic can obviously encourage us to pursue broader study on our own. If the critic can point out important relationships between films or discuss the body of a director's work, we can learn to do so too. The resources available are almost endless. A number of background books have been praised and recommended in these pages, and there will be more. This type of resource belongs in the home of the concerned Christian; it should also be a priority for church libraries.

We have remarked on the importance of the local church as a community of opinion and shared discipline. From this standpoint it is clear that a church library can be a tremendous asset. No church library should be without a copy of *Halliwell's Filmgoer's Companion*, Monaco's *How to Read a Film*, Knight's *The Liveliest Art*, or Capra's delightful autobiography, *The Name Above the Title*. Of course these could be supplemented with many other excellent works.

We should also remember that the church library is ideally suited for the collecting and lending of videos themselves. There are plenty of films that merit the direct investment of the church, especially children's videos. In addition, members can be encouraged to donate tapes they have bought or received as gifts.

Lending from a library is an excellent way to share the film experience, but church members have another option that is even better. That is actually sharing the movie as a group activity. Whether it is an independent fellowship or a traditional Sunday school class that schedules occasional movie nights, the possibilities are boundless. Many times after seeing a film, I am struck with how it would lend itself to group discussion. Peter Sellers's delightful *Heavens Above* and Allen's *Crimes and Misdemeanors* come to mind immediately, followed by *The Mission, Schindler's List, The Elephant Man, Black Robe* . . . I have to make myself stop. Every opportunity I have had to share films with church groups has reaffirmed this conviction. The group experience lets me draw on the insights of others who see from a better angle than I do on a given point. That's a tremendous advantage.

Take, for example, the viewing of a film like Bergman's *The Seventh Seal*. This famous work is rich in symbolism and weighted with concern for the most serious questions of life, death, and faith. Bergman has woven so much into his tapestry that he obviously is not addressing a casual, unthinking audience. The film demands a high level of concentration in the viewer, and a rather high level of cultural awareness. How much less intimidating and more interesting it becomes when an adult group can watch together: Maybe someone knows more than I do about life in the Middle Ages; another is familiar with medieval traditions like the Dance of Death; someone else is well-read in psychology and analysis. Last but not least would be someone (perhaps a pastor) with the right background to point out the theological implications of Bergman's filmscript. In a group setting the film will be more enjoyable for everybody. The process can be stimulating and rewarding, even if we don't all like the movie!

The more we learn about films and the great filmmakers, the more we will want to sample the treasures of our movie heritage. Fortunately, more and more classic films are appearing in video stores and on cable channels. It is up to us to claim them for our own experience. This is doubly important for Christian parents. While adults may have been exposed to the classics at some time in their lives, today's children grow up on a diet stuffed with the mediocrity of television.

Some young people are so conditioned by today's color-splashed TV that they are blocked from an appreciation of black-and-white films. We should recognize the advantage a young person gains simply by learning to enjoy black-and-white movies. Besides the fact that so many classics are in black and white, there are directors even today who maintain that black-and-white photography offers richer possibilities for the screen artist than color. A masterwork like *Schindler's List* is powerful evidence. But leaving Spielberg aside, recall the vivid impressions made by *The Grapes of Wrath, Citizen Kane, On the Waterfront, To Kill a Mockingbird,* all the great 30s films of Capra, Wyler, and Ford. The young person who grows up unable to respond to this tradition is disadvantaged indeed.

Conditions of the Movie Experience

Our care in finding the best movies to watch will be wasted if we do not give equal consideration to *how* we watch. Increased options in the form of videos and cable movies have raised greater challenges to our appreciation. The very abundance of a product can lead to careless habits in its use.

Much is determined by the simple choice of where to see a film: Do we catch it while it is still in the theaters, or do we wait till it comes out on video? There is more to consider here than simple economics. For those who are forced by necessity to find the least expensive solution, video rental will be the choice. For those not in this category it is wise to consider first the nature of the film.

Seeing a movie in the theater, as it was created to be seen, means seeing it in the optimum conditions of vividness, color balance, framing (wide-screen films are repackaged to fit the shape of the TV screen), and sound. The sound technology now available to filmmakers has the effect of enveloping us and drawing us into the world of the film. The darkness of the room and the absence of anything but the screen also reinforce the impact.

Unfortunately recent decades have witnessed the spread of poorly planned, second-rate theaters. The multiplex phenomenon has made it possible for many films to be seen at one location. It has also produced the abomination of the divided auditorium, where a spacious theater is halved by a concrete-block wall down the center. The resulting half-theaters often have problems with sound leakage and the relative size of the image; they should be avoided if possible.

However, when an adequate theater is available, it is always better to see a film projected on the large screen. In the aftermath of the VCR revolution, this point deserves special attention. Many people are in the habit of watching movies at home just because they can sprawl on the couch and dress negligibly. They never realize what they miss by making informality the sole criterion of their entertainment experience.

With schedules as crowded as they are nowadays, it is obvious that we can't see every good film while it is in the theaters. Thus it is wise to plan theater visits on the basis of a new criterion: Some movies by their nature demand viewing on the large screen, and some do not. All movies have a diminished impact when seen on a TV set, but some will suffer far more than others. It makes sense to catch the one type in the theater and (if necessary) wait for the other to come out on video.

Adventure movies and movies that involve outdoor spectacle of any kind (including scenic beauty) call for the full scale of a theater screen. Dramas, romances, and even police stories that use many interior scenes can be appreciated more adequately on the TV set. The real splendor of *Dances with Wolves* was in its visual treatment of the frontier via outdoor cinematography. On the other hand, *Driving Miss Daisy* and *My Left Foot* are more intimate and make for a much more satisfactory choice on video.

In regard to the dilemma of theater vs. home viewing, we might consider the value of so-called revival movie houses found in many communities. Such enterprises, existing on a modest budget in modest surroundings, often deserve our encouragement and patronage. Not only do they provide the film experience of projection on a large screen, but they also offer classics of the past that are still unavailable on video.

When there is nothing on at the theaters, or when other circumstances prevent going out, the alternative is to see a video at home. Here it becomes crucial that we follow good habits in preparation and selection. The investment of our time is important; the potential for reward and for disappointment is great.

Every time we select a video, we should do so on the basis of the best information available and the broadest awareness we can achieve. In general, the decision should always be made *before we enter a store*. If a choice is being made for two or more people, it should be discussed well beforehand. Browsing in a video store is fun, but in the long run the habit of careful selection prior to a visit will pay off.

Different approaches to the selection process work well for different people. In our house there is always a slip of paper somewhere with a short list of movies on it—like a grocery list. Trivial though it seems, this is an insurance policy to keep us aware of things that we really want to see. There are other good ways to provide insurance against hasty selections. Whatever the method, the important thing is preparation. This is another way to avoid the "Why-did-I-waste-my-time-on-that?" syndrome.

For Christians who use the VCR, it is essential to have at least one of the popular video guides. This is like having a reviewer on the shelf, with comments on any available video at your fingertips. As in reading a review, we need to use good judgment in following a guide. There is not one that will reflect our own taste unfailingly, or our Christian values. Fortunately, it is possible to get a sense of how your own viewpoint differs from that of the guide after using it a few times. The editors of the guide may have a weakness for screwball comedy that you do not share; they may feel that a certain director can do no wrong. As soon as you recognize this, you are that much better prepared to continue using the book with profit.

My wife and I like to keep more than one publication on hand in order to compare writeups. We have especially enjoyed the *Video Movie Guide* published yearly by Ballantine Books and edited by Mick Martin and Marsha Porter. The indexes for actors and for directors are an outstanding feature not found in many such directories. After we see a movie, we always enjoy checking the index to help us recall what other films a performer was in, or what else the director has done. This helps us to form a cumulative evaluation of the person's work, and from that to develop expectations for other films he or she has been a part of.

An even greater aid in this process is *Halliwell's Filmgoer's and Video Viewer's Companion.* The tenth edition of this work came out in 1993; such longevity reflects the satisfaction that the book has given its readers through the years. It is an alphabetically arranged thumbnail encyclopedia, with entries on every major performer, director, screenwriter, movie genre, etc. (Note, the *Companion* is not to be confused with the *Film Guide* which was also published by Halliwell.) There are brief movie quizzes sprinkled throughout, and an abundance of fascinating quotes from actors, directors, and other observers.

Another source that has given us pleasure and enlightenment is a little paperback called *Retakes*, by John Eastman. This book offers background information on the actual filming of some five hundred movies. There is more than the usual fan material about Tom Cruise driving his own race cars. One discovers here that William Wyler asked his players in *The Best Year of Our Lives* to wear their own clothes for filming; that *Places in the Heart* was filmed in the hometown of its creator, Robert Benton, and the Sally Fields role in the film was modeled after Benton's great-great-grandmother; that director Ralph Nelson offered his own home as collateral to finance *Lilies of the Field*. Understanding the challenges involved in filming and the great personal sacrifice that is sometimes required makes me appreciate a film more, even in retrospect.

How Not to Appreciate a Film

No two people respond to a movie, or a book or play, the same way. It is always a disappointment when we bring up a film that has meant something to us and find that for another person it was "just okay." I have found this to happen more frequently in the age of the VCR.

When someone else has seen a movie on video that I have enjoyed in the theater, I almost expect them to be less enthusiastic than I was. This is a natural by-product of the way television diminishes a film. However, there is often evidence that more has been lost than the mere difference in technology should warrant. Sometimes in discussing a worthwhile film I hear a person say, "It wasn't as good as people said it was," or perhaps, "I didn't understand all of it." On questioning, the speaker reveals some interesting details about his or her experience of the film, such as the following:

1) I only got involved when I came in from the grocery store and it was on, so I sat down to watch.

2) It looked like it was going to be good, but I had to leave in the middle to put the clothes in the dryer, and when I got back I could never get into it again.

3) We started it at 10:30, and I only got through an hour before I fell asleep.

Evidence such as this—and there are countless variations—comes up all too often when people talk about videos they have watched.

No wonder we fail to appreciate films! No wonder we miss the point! In such cases the very convenience we associate with the VCR works against its most effective use. These obstacles to meaningful viewing are spoken of as if they cannot be avoided. But do we have to accept all distractions as a matter of course? While a few will be inevitable, the majority are not so at all. They only happen if we let them.

What is too often missing is planning—or simple forethought. Household chores never *have to* be done at the same time we are watching a film. Game-playing by other family members does not *have to* occur in the same room with the TV set. We can schedule movie-watching at times that are clearly separate from committee meetings and trips to the grocery store. We can decide on a time and make it known so that those who want to see the movie can actually be there when it starts.

That some people let a variety of "unavoidable" events detract from the experience of movies points to one conclusion: They are treating movies the same way they treat television. With commercial TV it really doesn't matter when we do two things at once. We can watch while we iron, converse, or wash the cat. TV doesn't suffer because it is designed to engage only a small portion of our intelligence. The TV format takes us by the hand and leads us through its routine situations in a manner duplicated from night to night, week by week. The relentless commercial breaks invite us to relax our attention every few minutes, even if we are inclined to concentrate on a show.

Watching so many commercials affects the way we watch everything else; it helps to determine our expectations for all screen experiences. This effect can be harmful, since the ad people have such narrow goals. They don't care whether we really follow dialog, for example, or whether it makes sense, as long as an impression is made that will cause us to remember the brand. So when we don't pay attention to commercial television, it doesn't matter. The ad-makers *want* us to be lazy, slow-witted viewers.

In this respect movies—quality movies at least—are totally unlike television. We must know the difference if we are to benefit from watching movies with the VCR. The films that claim the attention of Christian viewers are not like elevator music or billboard art. They are designed to engage our senses of sight and hearing *and* to require all of our intelligence, not just a fraction as does television. Whoever refuses to recognize this difference might as well limit himself to television.

A movie worth watching is worth preparing to watch. This means planning a time in which we are not likely to be disturbed. It also means the discipline of controlling disturbances when they do occur. If family members enter the room after a movie has begun, they should have enough consideration not to interrupt the watchers with questions about what has happened or who is who. If talk is necessary, the movie should be stopped with a pause switch until the talk is completed. The family as a unit can develop the habit of respecting the movie watcher, and indeed those artists who have made the movies.

If the telephone rings, the film should be stopped until the call is dealt with. Leaving the room to answer a phone call is not a reason to return and distract other viewers with catch-up questions. That is what a pause button is for. (We should not be shy about asking if we can call back after the movie.)

Whenever interruptions do occur, it is important to return to the film as quickly as possible. No director plans a movie so that the audience can walk away and come back with a halt in projection. Movies are carefully structured to gain the effect of accumulated details. Each element builds on the other, and none should be missed. The sequences of the film are planned to unfold at a very definite pace from beginning to end. If we interfere with this progression, we are only robbing ourselves.

Completely in the Dark

There is more to consider in the way of preparation once the questions of scheduling and continuity are settled. We now face an important set of choices in regard to physical surroundings. The best way to enjoy a movie at home—and to be affected as it was designed to affect us—is to see that the viewing situation is as close to that of an actual theater as possible.

Movies have been offered in specialized, sometimes vastly expensive settings for three quarters of a century. When we see a film in a theater, we are in a closed room furnished with nothing but seats, curtains, and exit lights. There is not one distinctive object to look at besides the back of a head. Moreover, the room is darkened completely at the start of the movie; the only appreciable source of light is the screen image itself.

This elaborate effort to create the right environment is not a whim of theater owners. It is made for definite artistic reasons, and very good ones. Yet when it comes to the viewing of VCR movies, we often act as if we had never experienced a film in its proper setting before. There is no attention to extraneous noise, no thought taken for distance from the screen (which determines the size of the image we experience), and no consideration of the value of darkness.

By failing to manage the setting, we make ourselves vulnerable to a host of mental distractions throughout the watching of a film. At any moment the eye may wander from the riveting struggles of *The Miracle Worker* to the crooked picture on the wall that I meant to straighten two weeks ago, or from the tense drama of *Howard's End* to that pair of socks in the corner and why don't they ever do what you tell them with their dirty clothes?

Movies are not television. We must recognize the clash of TV habits with the habits demanded by film, and reject a TV-as-usual approach to the VCR.

So far we have only discussed conditions that exist while a movie is running. But it is possible for distractions that precede or follow a film to work against our full appreciation of it. An example is what usually happens at the end of a video movie: We see the words "The End," push a button, and immediately cut to an ongoing TV presentation. The TV show clashes with the ending of the film in mood, tempo, and meaning; in seconds it can obliterate whatever feelings the movie left us with.

By comparison, I can recall many occasions when I remained in my seat at a theater, letting the emotional impact of a movie sink in while other people filed out. Good movies can leave us charged with the power of their drama, and even of the ideas they contain. When we have this experience, there is available an immediate recall of certain lines, certain images, that will never be so fresh in the mind again. These after-moments are the perfect time to compare notes with others about events that may not have been clear, to share our appreciation of details that not everyone has caught.

For unwary viewers, the TV set can destroy these moments of savoring a film and enriching our appreciation of it. As soon as the rewind button is pressed, we can be thrown smack into a hockey game or a disaster report on the eleven o'clock news. It takes discipline to avoid this destructive intrusion. However, it can be done very simply by switching to a blank screen, deleting the sound, or best of all, turning the TV off completely while the VCR rewinds.

To sum up this chapter, we need only recall that movies do matter. They have the potential to give us experiences of lasting value, but to do so they require a serious effort from us. They have to be selected with care. They should be seen in the proper theater setting whenever possible. Watching them at home has its advantages, but there are a number of ways we can mar the experience as well. A carefully chosen film deserves viewing under the best possible conditions, even at home.

Christians can form habits that will insure the best results each time a movie is shown. The more we work on these habits of appreciation, the greater our pleasure and profit will be.

Notes to Chapter 11

1. Pauline Kael, "The 54th," *The New Yorker,* 5 February 1990, 111.

2. Judith Crist, *Take 22: Moviemakers on Moviemaking* (New York: Viking Penguin, 1984), 2.

DENNIS THE MENACE

"DO I SMELL POPCORN AND, IF NOT, **WHY** NOT?"

Chapter 12

Virtue and Praise

Finally, brethren, whatsoever things are true, whatsoever things are honest, whatsoever things are just, whatsoever things are pure, whatsoever things are lovely, whatsoever things are of good report; if there be any virtue, and if there be any praise, think on these things.
Philippians 4:8 (KJV)

It is time to focus on the positive; time to celebrate that moment when we slip a well-chosen film into the VCR, settle back with our loved ones, click the "play" button, and reach for the popcorn. And for this simple luxury, this ever-renewable expectation of pleasure, we can indeed praise the Lord!

One last word about preparation: A great viewing experience may come unexpectedly, but we make it more likely with planning. Movie watching benefits from reinforcement, and we can devise any number of methods to utilize this principle. One key is to find a linking element between quality movies, whether it is a subject, a director, a screenwriter, or something else that movies can have in common.

I get more out of a great Frank Capra film when I can relate it to other Capra films I have enjoyed. If I discover that Preston Sturges was in some ways the heir of Capra, then a valuable new avenue opens up for me to explore. Part of my enjoyment of a Sturges movie like *Sullivan's Travels* will lie in recognizing how Sturges is like Capra and how he is unique.

A good linking element among films can be like a vein of gold waiting to be followed and mined. We can discover links of quality based on an endless variety of elements. Movie treatments of the novels of a single author make for fascinating comparisons. Or one might savor the vast legacy of biographies on film. Broader realms for exploration are the classics of the silent era, the films of the 1930s (why were there so many good ones made then?) and foreign films—even those of a particular nation.

The VCR offers welcome alternatives to the usual Hollywood product. We now have access to the best work coming from Australia and the United Kingdom, such as *Gallipoli, Local Hero, The Shooting Party, Hear My Song,* and *Enchanted April.* Nor should we pass up the rich offerings of non-English-speaking countries. Works like *Cinema Paradiso, Das Boot, The Return of Martin Guerre, Au Revoir les Enfants,* and *My Father's Glory* (with its sequel *My Mother's Castle*) cannot be recommended too highly. Any of a half-dozen masterworks by Kurosawa will demonstrate why his genius has inspired so many American directors.

Of course the principle of association is not foolproof. There will always be disappointments. No matter how carefully we choose, or how highly someone else recommends a movie, it still may turn out to be a bust. In some instances it just isn't the right time for a particular movie, no matter how good. But none of this should keep us from expecting great things from a well-chosen film.

The movies discussed in the remainder of this chapter will repay the highest expectations. They are representative of many others that we have not space to include. Although some are recognized as classics, they do not define any standard of artistic excellence. Rather, they suggest possibilities for the presentation of Christian values in films of all types. To avoid any suggestion of priority, they have been placed in alphabetical order.

Each of these movies offers something special. As always, to find that something we have to be looking.

Babette's Feast

This movie gives us the most sensitive treatment on film of religious commitment as it affects family relationships. It tells two stories in one. The primary plot involves a nineteenth-century Danish pastor, who is widowed, and his two grown daughters. They are members of a Lutheran sect distinguished by its austere life of self-denial. Rarely does a movie take such persons as its subject; to depict them with the sympathy and respect of *Babette's Feast* is remarkable.

The story of the pastor's family examines the stresses that result when each daughter has her chance to leave home for a husband and a new life. The suitor in each case represents the secular world that the father rejects. We do not see in these dilemmas a struggle for freedom from tyranny, which they would become in most contemporary films. The ruling factor in each case is love, and love in a Christian form, where we place the good of the other person above our own good. This kind of love (largely unknown in Hollywood) doesn't make for winners and losers—it has its rewards for all.

But this is only the first of the two stories, and it is the second—the story of Babette—that adds sparkle to the whole. The Danish family represent Protestant severity; Babette arrives as a refugee from political turmoil in France and becomes the symbol of a quite different outlook. She has been a celebrated beauty in a Paris that was devoted to pleasure and extravagance. While the Danish family has a limited awareness of sensual experience, she has had it all.

Babette is chastened after her flight from France; and as friendship with the two Danish women blossoms, we see that she is capable of a self-giving love. She too earns the dignity of self-denial in her gracious acceptance of circumstances. The interweaving of the lives of such different personalities is fascinating and full of surprising twists.

The twist that gives the film its title also provides a wonderful climax to the two stories. The banquet is a perfect symbol of how the good things of life can become a means for the expression and the sharing of love. It is an ancient theme given a glorious new treatment.

Few of us in the audience will share the outlook of the father in all its severity. Neither does the filmmaker, but he treats the old pastor's faith and works with absolute respect. And this enables him to fashion a poignant, gripping, and in the end jubilant movie experience.

Breaker Morant
Based on actual events, *Breaker Morant* displays excellence at many levels. The taut screenplay creates a courtroom drama to equal *Witness for the Prosecution* or *Anatomy of a Murder*. Director Bruce Beresford has made good choices at every turn, and the cast is outstanding.

The story involves a group of Australian soldiers fighting in Africa during the Boer War. They are part of an irregular British force formed to deal with the guerilla tactics of the Dutch frontier fighters. It is unconventional warfare, and terrible things are done on both sides. The central characters are trapped between the demand for success and the demand that they go by the book, as their British superiors interpret it.

In the pivotal incident, a detachment of the Australians is ambushed (under extremely suspicious circumstances) and its popular commander killed. The unit then goes about getting revenge under his successor, Captain Morant. Rules are broken, as they have been all along, but now it serves diplomatic ends to make a show of punishing the Australians.

Plot elements, direction, and acting make *Breaker Morant* a great film. But there is more that makes it an important movie for Christians to see. It is a story of justice sought for a few individuals, but their experience reflects the moral commitments of a whole society. What is on trial in the hot South African military compound is, not just three unlucky Australian soldiers, but the British Empire. And by a logical extension Western society—the Christian world, as it then thought of itself.

The Australian volunteers in South Africa, like a lot of soldiers throughout history, have little idea of why they are there. The sense of dislocation is subtly conveyed by a scene at an encampment on the veldt. A guard gives the order for lights-out, and then calls for three cheers for King Edward. The soldiers dutifully respond from within their tents; muffled cheers rise and then die away. The tents and the silence remain under the darkening African sky. None of these soldiers will ever see an English monarch, but they are here in Africa to kill and die for the Empire.

What the king of England represented, among other things, was a dominant world order that claimed Christianity as its foundation. The king was crowned in a Christian shrine with rites derived from the Christian ecclesiastical tradition. The opposing sides in the Boer War—British forces and Dutch settlers alike—thought of themselves as representing Christian nations, in contrast to the pagan societies of Africa.

The Christian background and the historical circumstances pertaining to it are indicated with sublety and skill. Christian missionaries are involved in the strife between the two factions, and are even implicated in espionage. During the trial the examiners question whether a certain act was a Christian thing to do. In the final scene the protagonists point up the contrast between Christian and pagan cultures with stunning irony.

At the heart of *Breaker Morant* lie profound questions: What kind of world were these so-called Christian nations building when they came to Africa (and to other continents)? And what legacy do Christian societies create when so much of their national striving is done in God's name?

To the movie's credit, these questions are not spelled out for us. There is no preaching of liberal or conservative doctrines such as we often find in Hollywood films. For many viewers *Breaker Morant* will not be a superb drama, a suspenseful whodunnit. And that's all right. But the deeper questions are there for thoughtful viewers—above all thoughtful Christians—to recognize and ponder.

This movie provides neither a crude attack on Western traditions nor a simple-minded defense of them. It just makes us think. And it was never more important to think about these things than it is today—things like the role of Christianity in the structure and aims of a society, or the demands of Christian behavior when they conflict with the political context. Films like *Breaker Morant* help us to understand who we are as heirs of an imperfect history. We could use a lot more of them.

Hobson's Choice

This 1954 comedy by David Lean represents the best of the British film tradition. Even Pauline Kael, one of the sternest of critics, mentions the old-fashioned impulse to applaud when we see this one.

Hobson's Choice is a worthy example of Lean's directorial achievement. (Many critics prefer his early films to the later epics like *Doctor Zhivago.*) The settings—the mise-en-scène—beautifully recreate turn-of-the-century industrial Lancashire. The use of the camera is remarkably effective. For example, we may be well into a scene when the camera pulls back to reveal something in the foreground of which we were unaware. There are fine examples of an effect called the *subjective camera,* when the lens sees the world just as the character does (Hobson's double vision when he is drunk).

The preeminent attraction of the film is the acting of the three principals: Brenda de Banzie, John Mills, and Charles Laughton. De Banzie gives a fantastic performance as Hobson's oldest daughter, Maggie—a woman who decides to stand up for herself in the male-dominated

Victorian setting. The wonder of her performance is that she conveys such redoubtable strength and determination and still remains a warm-hearted, thoroughly appealing woman. (She is a terrific role model for today's sophisticated young people.) Maggie defies her father, over-throwing his tyranny, yet still loves him in a deeper way than he deserves.

John Mills, a mainstay of British cinema in the 50s, almost equals de Banzie's performance in the way he portrays a young man who grows from nobody into a self-respecting adult. Early on he captures perfectly Willie's shyness and naiveté. He hardly knows what to do with himself when they let him out of the cellar where he makes shoes for Hobson's shop. But Mills is totally believable as he grows into this new self, justifying Maggie's faith in him.

These performances by Mills and de Banzie may just be better than Laughton's. But then Charles Laughton is Charles Laughton, and this will always be thought of as a Laughton film, along with others, like *Mutiny on the Bounty* or *Ruggles of Red Gap*.

Laughton was an actor from the old school who sailed into a perform-ance with all flags flying. Sometimes there was too much of it, but in roles like this one he is wonderful. One secret of Hobson is the very real selfishness of the character. If he were sugared over as many screen rascals are, the movie would be cheapened by half. But Laughton is a great enough scoundrel to call forth genuine heroism in Maggie and Willie, when the three of them do battle.

The final distinction of *Hobson's Choice* is its quality as a love story. It torpedoes the mindless assumptions about romantic love that now per-vade movies. In the standard Hollywood doctrine love is no more than an accident: People "find" love the way they find a parking place at the mall. How do they know it's love? Because it *feels* so right . . . until next time.

Hobson's Choice demonstrates to young people the radical concept that love is a choice you make, and then make successful. Maggie *decides* to love Willie (she knows him well already) and then commits herself to following through on that decision, day after day. In the process she becomes changed as she helps Willie to change.

Only superficially does she "make him over." More than that, she inspires him and puts him in touch with his own possibilities. The picture of her giving him his writing lesson (he is illiterate at first)—under-standing his deficiency but not making a big deal out of it—is one of the great moments in the film. There are lots more for the lucky people who see this movie.

Holiday

Ours is a time when the striving for wealth and power is the most revered principle of life. Witness the glamor of the deal-maker and the steady growth of the law student population. Yet we have always know that the focus on material success is radically anti-Christian. On no point did Jesus speak more plainly or more forcefully.

George Cukor's 1935 comedy *Holiday* is a delightful antidote for the wealth-and-power virus. It offers something extra to teenagers with its insight into the problem of discovering the right partner in life. Cary Grant plays a young man on the threshold of a life of success as the world defines it. Talented and industrious, he is about to marry into a wealthy family that will sponsor and guarantee his rise. His fiancee is the older daughter, who professes to love him for what he is, but clearly intends to love him for the way he will suit her goals and her lifestyle. She means well—she knows how beneficial her influence will be! Her smugness and condescension make her the opposite of Maggie in *Hobson's Choice*.

Though the movie is a very funny comedy, it brings into sharp focus those still-powerful pressures to conform to the world's expectations. Grant is a wonderfully effective protagonist as he hesitates between making his fiancee (and her family) happy and holding onto his own values and goals.

Then there's the other daughter, played incomparably by Katherine Hepburn. Though she loves her parents and sister, she doesn't share their self-centered outlook. She recognizes the true nature of Grant from the beginning and longs to save him from his fate. Her inner struggle between family loyalty and the love she feels for Grant (plain to the audience if to no one else) is a compelling drama in itself. I am not one who finds Hepburn irresistible in every movie she made, but in a handful like this one her talent is something to behold—you just can't imagine anyone else doing the part.

Seen today, this film suggests interesting parallels to *The Graduate,* with its intense conflict between generations. *Holiday* may have been before its time, or it may prove that the problem of holding onto ones values while choosing a path in life is an eternal one, as old as Abraham and Lot.

Innocent and old-fashioned as it is compared to *The Graduate, Holiday* is still a wiser and more mature film.

Lilies of the Field

Here is a perfect example of the so-called "little" film that can pack more energy and more spiritual power than half a dozen major productions. (Director Ralph Nelson shot this one in fourteen days, using his own home as collateral for the financing.) If anyone expects this story from the 60s to be dated or naive, he or she is in for a surprise. *Lilies of the Field* just gets better with age.

The story takes place in the American Southwest. A group of nuns from eastern Europe have escaped over the Berlin Wall and now occupy a plot of land that was somehow donated to their order. One hot summer day a stranger pulls in off the highway to get water for his radiator. The mother superior raises her eyes heavenward with a prayer of thanks that God has sent her this "big, strong man." Right away we start to guess what's in store for the traveller.

In relating how the nuns try to get Homer Smith (Sidney Poitier) to build a chapel for them, the story unfolds with the inevitability of a parable. There is a distinct echo of the Old Testament story of Jonah in the hero's reluctance. In fact, the entire screenplay is rich with biblical references, both direct and indirect.

There is much fun along the way in the conflict between Poitier's down-home baptist Homer and the Old-world Catholics. But the movie excels in its penetrating case studies of Christian behavior. We get telling glimpses of Mother Maria's struggles with herself when Homer calls her to account for her dictatorial methods (he compares her to Hitler!). Homer's own difficulties are more typical of most Christians; for example, not wanting to abandon our own plans and give ourselves up to God for his purposes. Or once we have begun a good work, not being willing to let others join in and share the credit.

It is true that a movie character like Homer would be written and played differently today. He'd be less nice, more nitty-gritty. (Imagine— Poitier says "damn" one time in the entire movie.) But Poitier invests this idealized role with a zest and humor that show why he made such an impact in the 60s. This is what reviewers mean when they refer to a star as "magnetic."

If for no other reason, the movie would be worth seeing for the front porch song session where German nuns meet Georgia gospel. You may end up clapping your hands and singing with them . . . *Amen!*

A Man for All Seasons

We always admire a well-made film about courage under fire. In this category there have been some great ones, often dealing with people willing to die for what they believe. *A Man for All Seasons* stands out among them because it shows us that sometimes more is necessary than even courage. To serve God truly, we need, not just to be strong, but to be strong wisely.

Robert Bolt's screenplay about the career of Thomas More (based on his own stage play) is a classic. With its brilliant exposition and plotting, the drama grips like a wrench as we witness the inexorable closing-in of More's enemies. But there is another drama more subtle and more profound than these desperate political maneuverings. It is played out within the mind of the hero.

Sir Thomas More is a great man, but he is a frightened, troubled man burdened with anxiety for his loved ones and his country. The reign of Henry VIII in England was a time of confusion, hypocrisy and bizarre changes of policy. More's heroism lies in his commitment to knowing exactly where he stands amid all this upheaval. He is determined to see if his own ground is sure, and to measure exactly what is required of him from one situation to the next.

As Bolt presents him, More is a man who makes it his business to *see clearly,* to understand any threat to his faith before he reacts. This eliminates the easy way out taken by most of his colleagues, and likely most of us: that is, to make sure we are unaware of what's going on, and especially of all the implications, until after it's too late to do anything.

The New Testament principle of loving one's enemies is woven throughout the drama. It is illustrated in the contrast between More and various other characters, especially his hot-headed son-in-law, Will Roper. Roper's defiance of authority is basically an adolescent outpouring of emotion, not the product of prayer and carefully reasoned thought that is More's. Yet Thomas is constantly charged with being unreasonable. He confounds both friends and enemies by taking the precepts of Christ literally. The story of his struggle leaves us with a simple illustration of

Matthew 16:25: "For whosoever will save his life shall lose it: and whosoever will lose his life for my sake shall find it" (KJV).

The moral impact of this film is so strong that we tend to forget its excellence from any other standpoint. Happily, it is a rare example of worthy matter matched with great artistry. The starting point is Bolt's screenplay, which is served tastefully and creatively by the director (Fred Zinneman, who won the Academy Award). There is so much in this script that the movie deserves two or three viewings so that every point may have its impact.

The acting is of such a high caliber that we see repeated viewings with undiminished pleasure. Paul Scofield's Academy Award–winning performance is unforgettable. But for me the glory of the film is its gallery of supporting players: Orson Welles capping his career as Cardinal Wolsey; the great Wendy Hiller in a moving performance as More's wife, Alice; Leo McKern a deadly antagonist as Thomas Cromwell; and Robert Shaw almost perfect as Henry VIII. This is only the beginning of the list.

A Man for All Seasons is unquestionably a movie for all Christians. It is a monument whose outlines become more impressive as the years go by.

The Man from Snowy River

This movie would even convince my dad that they do sometimes make them like they used to. It does not aspire to be great cinema art, but it manages to be just about the most likable movie I know.

Lots of people had recommended this film to me before I had a chance to see it. One thing they all stressed was that this is a movie *everyone* will enjoy. They were right. A pleasure for any adult, it is even more valuable for young people because they will identify with the two central characters.

In recent years Hollywood has displayed an obsession with coming of age. It is an ancient and honorable theme. But many filmmakers seem to have decided that it means only one thing—having a sexual experience with someone older and (supposedly) wiser. Consider the evidence going back to *The Graduate* (1968) and *Summer of '42*, which came out in 1972. At first it was always a male who was initiated by an older woman, but predictably in recent years the urgent problem has been for young women to escape the burden of virginity. The pseudogenteel *Dirty Dancing* is an example.

This type of movie is promoted and admired on the basis of an inadequate but widely accepted notion: that to "become a man" or to "become a woman" means just having sex for the first time. In some versions it is refined to mean having sex for the first time when it actually *felt right*. There is not a more specious doctrine in all of screen entertainment.

The Man from Snowy River proceeds on the sturdy assumption that more things go into the making of a man or woman than a hop into the haystack. The movie is about the attainment of adulthood, and in its treatment of the subject it is simply splendid. Two young people in frontier Australia (Tom Burlinson and Sigrid Thornton) are forced to make the kind of choices that will determine the course of the future, and will in fact define the persons they become. The process is difficult, and they make mistakes along the way. But ultimately they make the right choices. Their behavior is responsible both to themselves and to the adults who stand in a parental relationship to them.

A special virtue of this film is the way it suggests that a person can rarely make it on his own. We depend on the help and guidance of others if we are to gain fulfillment. My favorite scene comes when the young hero gives up on an adult community that has treated him unfairly, and heads back to the mountains in disgust. He is joined at this campfire by a couple of long-time adult friends, who offer some wise and tactful advice. His mentor, Clancy (played by Jack Thompson), hits on the central question: "What is the first thing you do when a horse has thrown you?" The young man knows you have to get back on again, and right away. He soon realizes that he must go back and learn to live in society, with all its flaws.

A lot of movies aimed at today's teen audience simply pander to the egotism of youth. They present a stereotyped world of conflict between sincere, spontaneous young people and narrow-minded if not dim-witted adults. In contrast, *The Man from Snowy River* gives us an impressive group of sympathetic adults. The understanding and support of friends like Clancy and Thornton's aunt suggest a whole human community that can help young people overcome the prejudice and fear embodied in Thornton's father (Kirk Douglas).

The Man from Snowy River is not to be critiqued on the basis of dramatic realism. It follows the tradition of Walter Scott and Robert Louis Stevenson in stretching the limits of probability. But this is only in regard to incidents of the plot, where we are usually indulgent for the sake of entertainment. In the more vital areas of emotional and psychological credibility, the film is refreshingly honest.

P.S. The sequel to this movie, called *Return to Snowy River,* is an enjoyable adventure romance. It does not match the original in story interest or characterization. The appeal of the first film lies in the growth of the young hero and heroine; in the second, there is nowhere for the characters to go. We still get plenty of gorgeous scenery and more exciting footage of the running horses (is there any more splendid subject for motion-picture photography?). But don't watch *Return* until you have seen the original.

The Mission

To compare *The Mission* with *A Man for All Seasons* involves a leap from the heart of the Old World into the jungle wilderness of the New. But these two films have important points in common, which is not surprising since both were scripted by Robert Bolt. Like its predecessor, *The Mission* centers on a conflict between individual Christian commitment and official Church policy. It too offers more than a simple morality tale of innocence versus evil.

Based on historical fact, *The Mission* fulfills its promise as a drama of martyrdom and an inspiring story of faith. The pleasure it affords is enhanced by the visual splendor of its jungle setting. A ravishing score by veteran film composer Ennio Morricone complements the spectacular scenery. (This is another of those films that beg to be seen in a theater, not on a small screen.)

With all of its impressive technical elements, *The Mission* achieves distinction because it strikes an unusual balance in the emotional give and take of its story. We identify fully with its central hero, but the film draws a more complete picture by involving us in the aims and the logic of the opposition. Not only that, it provides two different heroes so that the moral dilemma is complicated by the disagreement of the protagonists. The resulting drama is so intense that we have to remind ourselves it is based on fact.

Jeremy Irons plays the primary role of an idealistic, wholly committed Jesuit priest who devotes his life to ministry among the natives. Robert

De Niro has the showier role of a convert who changes from despicable slave trader to enthusiastic worker among the flock. The period is the seventeenth century.

The central historic conflict develops when the Catholic hierarchy decides to eliminate the mission that the priests have so lovingly and painstakingly developed. The move is transparently political, and the headstrong De Niro character is unable to acquiesce as Irons chooses to do. The tragic struggle between these two good men illustrates conflicts such as Christians have wrestled with for centuries. It raises the disturbing question: How many of us really believe it is better to turn the other cheek when faced with unjust action? How well have Christians ever understood the Lord's message that "Vengeance is mine, I will repay?"

One thing that clearly distinguishes the modern era from earlier periods like that of *The Mission* is our focus on life in this world. We measure success in the present tense, by tangible results. Life in eternity is uniformly disregarded. Yet the opposite emphasis is a key element of New Testament belief.

The Mission sets before us a vivid test of our faith on this point. The hero meets with disaster in human terms. We respond with shock and pity, perhaps even outrage. But I wonder what the feeling of the real missionaries was in this case. Did they understand better than we do what Jesus meant when he said, "He that loses his life for my sake will find it"?

A final distinctive feature of *The Mission* is the way it involves us in the moral inertia of the church bureaucracy. This works mainly through the character of the emissary from the Vatican, played skillfully by Phillip Bosco. He becomes even more interesting dramatically than the two priests who initiate the action. He is intelligent, observant, and even sympathetic, but his deepest commitment is to the status quo. He has none of the passion or the love that motivate the missionaries. But he is not without regret for his actions; that he can see no other way to proceed is part of the tragedy.

If we are honest, we may recognize that we are more like him than we are like the missionaries. Be sure to watch the film all the way through the closing credits, for it is the emissary that we see last. He gazes steadfastly out at us, as if to ask, "Would you have done any differently?"

Tender Mercies

One of those names that we can rely on as a mark of quality in a film is that of screenwriter Horton Foote. An Oscar winner in 1962 for the screenplay of *To Kill a Mockingbird,* he has won praise more recently for features such as *The Trip to Bountiful. Tender Mercies* displays his consistent dedication to themes that Christian viewers cherish, among them the power of love in reconstructing human wreckage.

The film is a milestone for director Bruce Beresford, who takes on an American subject in an American setting for the first time. It presents the story of a broken man's struggle for redemption. This has always been a popular concept in Hollywood, and never more than in recent years, as evidenced by such examples as *The Fisher King, The Doctor,* and *City of Joy.*

In this instance Beresford has the considerable advantage of Robert Duvall in the lead role, with an excellent ensemble surrounding him. Foote's screenplay is an honest and unpretentious look at how life is lived in areas of the U.S. that are remote from our big cities. What makes the movie unique is the way Beresford and his actors take the characters on their own terms. These are plain folk from top to bottom (though the Duvall character has known success and celebrity as a singer and song-writer), but there is not a hint of condescension toward them. Their lives are important, and the values they hold are honored without equivocation.

Tess Harper excels as the woman who falls in love with the drifting Duvall. In her character we see an overflowing love, but also a recognition that love cannot flourish without responsibility. An essential element in this characterization is her Christian faith, supported by her church and her pastor. The transformation of Mac Sledge (Duvall) is inevitably signified by his appearance at church with Harper and her son.

The initial church visit leads to an interesting moment when the pastor greets Mac and invites him to get involved. For a second I expected another distorted movie portrait of a hypocritical, glad-handing preacher. I was mistaken. This minister is so unaffected that you wonder if he is not a real pastor recruited by Beresford on location.

The quiet but unshakable faith of the woman registers throughout the movie. There is no question that her love for Mac—and the strength she offers him which is grounded in her faith—are the things that transform his life. The seriousness of the film is evident in a single unusual fact: While Mac has come to live on the place with this young widow, and while they do fall in love, there are no sex scenes. What this movie is about is too important for that.

Don't let all this attention to values give you the impression that *Tender Mercies* is sober or dull. It's a good story told in a richly satisfying film. You'll want to savor it more than once.

You Can't Take it With You

Frank Capra was not a realist. He was criticized even during his lifetime for painting a false picture of life's possibilities. Marxist critics, in particular, found him intolerable. They charged that his films misled the lower class audience. Those popular comedies persuaded them that happiness could be attained in other ways than the overthrow of the system. Capra was a menace: He was guilty of wanting redemption for everybody, both high and low!

The greatest Capra films were those made in the 30s, especially when they paired Jean Arthur with either Gary Cooper or James Stewart. These collaborations rank with *It Happened One Night* as Capra's finest. The latter film established the pattern of the screwball comedy, perhaps the most successful genre in movie history.

In a sense, to discuss one Capra film is to discuss them all, because the sincerity and idealism were so consistent in his work. However, as with most artists, there were also changes from one period to another. World War II interrupted Capra's career at its height, as it did with many of Hollywood's greatest. The war experience changed the nation profoundly, and Capra was never as perfectly attuned to the needs and conflicts of postwar America as he had been before. The real magic is in the early films.

Capra's first movie with James Stewart, *You Can't Take it With You*, provides a delectable combination of his moral themes and his typical characters and settings. It includes an element of whimsy that was common to many films of the period. Even with the occasional goofiness, Capra's sure instinct for comedy guides this film briskly to its conclusion. As in all of his films after *Mr. Deeds Goes to Town* (1936), the fun is mixed with deeper meditations on good and evil, and how we should all live in a democracy.

When movie guides refer to *You Can't Take it With You*, they always mention the oddball household of Grandpa Vanderhof, the wise patriarch played by Lionel Barrymore. It is indeed a looney bunch of characters, but lovable characters as only Capra could make them. Their world of innocence and good intentions is contrasted sharply with the world of "reality" represented by a hard-edged businessman named Kirby (Edward Arnold). The two worlds collide when a Kirby business scheme threatens to run the Vanderhofs out of their home. In fine Shakespearian fashion, the families are embroiled when Kirby's son (Stewart) falls for Grandpa Vanderhof's warm, intelligent granddaughter (Jean Arthur).

Despite the rewards of watching the young Stewart and Arthur, the movie belongs to Barrymore and Arnold. Kirby, whose wealth has been acquired in banking and munitions, stands opposed to Vanderhof in the values they represent. This conflict is echoed effectively *within* the character of Kirby as Arnold plays him. He gradually responds to the influence of Vanderhof and the effect that the Vanderhof household has on his son. Kirby begins as a character confirmed in selfishness and cynicism; Arnold makes his ultimate transformation believable even when it occurs within a rather outlandish plot twist.

Viewing a Capra film today does call for a bit of indulgence for the sentimentality he could draw on. This is sometimes sneered at as "Capracorn." There is always a conflict between this sentimentality and his sharp, intelligent criticism of social evil. His best pictures hold the two elements in balance, and leaven the mix with irresistible comedy.

It is true that Capra was a myth maker. In all of his major films he fashions a central myth that seems inconsistent with the facts of modern life. The myth involves an ideal, represented by persons like Grandpa Vanderhof and Gary Cooper's Longfellow Deeds. Their world is a classless community of brotherly love, one that is radically different from the so-called real world. But Capra's heroes see through the fraud of the real world and its values. People like Mr. Deeds, Mr. Smith, and Vanderhof know what is important and real in life, and it's not money.

So maybe Capra's form of myth-making is important. If we don't carry in our hearts a vital image of what life should be, we will fall victim to apathy and complacency about what it is. We will be duped by those more conventional myths about wealth and self-aggrandizement that the world finds so persuasive. These are the myths that are truly dangerous.

Listing the merits of a wonderful movie is always a pleasure. But citing a hand-picked group as we have done here can produce a reaction. The doubters will point out that we covered over fifty years to come up with these ten. Just how many others are there? they will ask. And more to the point, how easy will it be to get at them?

I admire a healthy skeptic, but here the evidence is on the side of optimism. The past couple of years have yielded films of undeniable excellence: *Enchanted April, Gettysburg, The Remains of the Day, Shadowlands, Schindler's List,* and more. But the best thing about the current situation is that the most talented and most serious of today's artists are just hitting their stride. We can expect much more from the likes of Spielberg, Beresford, Kenneth Branagh, and Emma Thompson. It is exciting to contemplate what may be in store for us in coming years.

When the next masterpiece appears, don't let us say to ourselves, "It will never play in our town." With the spread of videa outlets and the accelerated development of cable movie delivery, there is just not much that we have to miss. Keep in mind that we can make the market. If you don't see a movie like *Babette's Feast* or *Mr. Smith Goes to Washington* at your local store, ask for it. If you get no encouragement, go and tell your Sunday school class and other Christian friends. When that video renter gets the second or third request, you can bet he'll be reaching for his catalog. And public libraries are always eager for suggestions.

Remember, the better you prepare yourself to appreciate movies, the more you will enjoy them and the more meaningful they will be. And when you realize you've missed something really good at the theater, don't just write it off. One of the great things about great movies is that they are *still there.* You can see them again at a theater near you . . . even if that happens to be your own living room!

Selected Bibliography

Berg, A. Scott. *Goldwyn: A Biography*. New York: Balantine Books, 1990.

Bergman, Andrew. *We're in the Money: Depression America and Its Films*. New York: Harper & Row, 1972.

Bergman, Ingmar. *The Magic Lantern: An Autobiography*. Translated by Joan Tate. New York: Viking Penguin, 1988.

Bettelheim, Bruno. *The Uses of Enchantment: The Meaning and Importance of Fairy Tales*. New York: Vintage Books, a Division of Random House, 1977.

Bogdanovich, Peter. *John Ford*. Studio Vista Series. London: Movie Magazine Limited, 1967.

Bobker, Lee R. *Elements of Film*. 3rd edition. New York: Harcourt Brace Jovanovich, 1979.

Boorstin, Daniel J. *The Image: A Guide to Pseudo-Events in America*. New York: Atheneum, 1972.

Boyum, Joy Gould. *Double Exposure: Fiction Into Film*. New York: New American Library, 1989.

Campbell, Joseph. *The Hero with a Thousand Faces*. Bollinger Series XVII. Princeton, N.J.: Princeton University Press, 1972.

Capra, Frank. *The Name Above the Title: An Autobiography*. New York: Vintage Books, a Division of Random House, 1985.

Carlyle, Thomas. *On Heroes, Hero-Worship and the Heroic in History*. Originally published 1841. The World's Classics. London: Oxford University Press, 1965.

Crist, Judith. *Take 22: Moviemakers on Moviemaking*. New York: Viking Penguin, 1984.

Earley, Steven C. *An Introduction to American Movies*. New York: New American Library, 1978.

Eastman, John. *Retakes: Behind the Scenes of 500 Classic Movies*. New York: Ballantine Books, 1989.

Eyles, Allen. *James Stewart*. New York: Stein and Day, 1984.

Gardner, John. *On Moral Fiction*. New York: Basic Books, 1978.

Gianetti, Louis D. *Understanding Movies*. 5th edition. Englewood Cliffs, N.J.: Prentice Hall, 1990.

Greene, Graham. *The Pleasure Dome*. Oxford: Oxford University Press, 1980.

Halliwell, Leslie. *Halliwell's Filmgoer's and Video Viewer's Companion*. Edited by John Walker. 10th edition. New York: HarperCollins, 1993.

Haskell, Molly. *From Reverence to Rape: The Treatment of Women in the Movies*. 2nd edition. Chicago: University of Chicago Press, 1987.

Jacobs, Lewis. *The Rise of the American Film*. New York: Harcourt, Brace, 1939; reprint, New York: Teachers College Press, 1968.

Katz, Ephraim. *The Film Encyclopedia*. Perigee Books. New York: Putnam Publishing Group, 1982.

Kael, Pauline. *I Lost It At the Movies*. New York: Bantam Books, 1966.

_____. *Kiss Kiss, Bang Bang*. Boston: Little, Brown, 1968.

Kelley, Michael R. *A Parent's Guide to Television: Making the Most of it*. New York: John Wiley and Sons, 1983.

Kendall, Elizabeth. *The Runaway Bride: Hollywood Romantic Comedy of the 1930s*. New York: Alfred A. Knopf, 1990.

Knight, Arthur. *The Liveliest Art: A Panoramic History of the Movies*. Revised edition. New York: New American Library, 1979.

Koury, Phil A. *Yes, Mr. DeMille*. New York: G. P. Putnam's Sons, 1959.

Leff, Leonard J. and Jerold L. Simmons. *The Dame In The Kimono: Hollywood, Censorship and the Production Code from the 1920s to the 1960s*. New York: Grove Weidenfeld, 1990.

McBride, Joseph, ed. *Focus on Howard Hawks*. Englewood Cliffs, N.J.: Prentice Hall, 1972.

McKibben, Bill. *The Age of Missing Information*. New York: Random House, 1992.

Martin, Mick and Marsha Porter. *Video Movie Guide 1992*. New York: Ballantine Books, 1991. (New edition published yearly.)

Mast, Gerald and Marshall Cohen, eds. *Film Theory and Criticism: Introductory Readings*. 3rd edition. New York: Oxford University Press, 1985.

Medved, Michael. *Hollywood vs. America: Popular Culture and the War on Traditional Values*. New York: HarperCollins Publishers, 1992.

Menninger, Karl, M.D. *Whatever Became of Sin?* New York: Hawthorn Books, 1973.

Miller, Mark Crispin, ed. *Seeing Through Movies*. New York: Pantheon Books, 1990.

Monaco, James. *How to Read a Film*. Revised edition. New York: Oxford University Press, 1981.

Murray, Edward. *Nine American Film Critics*. New York: Frederick Ungar, 1975.

Postman, Neil. *Amusing Ourselves to Death: Public Discourse in the Age of Show Business*. New York: Penguin Books, 1986.

Ray, Robert B. *A Certain Tendency of the Hollywood Cinema, 1930–1980*. Princeton, N.J.: Princeton University Press, 1985.

Rutstein, Nat. *Go Watch TV!* New York: Sheed and Ward, 1974.

Ryken, Leland. *The Liberated Imagination: Thinking Christianly about the Arts*. Wheaton, Illinois: Harold Shaw Publishers, 1989.

Schatz, Thomas. *The Genius of the System: Hollywood Filmmaking in the Studio Era*. New York: Pantheon Books, 1988.

Schickel, Richard. *Schickel on Film*. New York: William Morrow, 1989.

Schrag, Robert L. *Taming the Wild Tube: A Family's Guide to Television and Video*. Chapel Hill: University of North Carolina Press, 1990.

Selznick, David O. *Memo from David O. Selznick*. Edited by Rudy Behmer. New York: Viking Press, 1972.

Shepherd, Donald and Robert Slatzer with Dave Grayson. *Duke: The Life and Times of John Wayne*. Garden City, N.Y.: Doubleday, 1985.

Sklar, Robert. *Movie-Made America: A Cultural History of American Movies*. New York: Vintage Books, a Division of Random House, 1975.

Skornia, Harry J. *Television and Society*. New York: McGraw-Hill, 1965.

Stephenson, Ralph and J. R. Debrix. *The Cinema as Art*. Harmondsworth: Penguin Books, 1965.

Thomson, David. *America in the Dark: The Impact of Hollywood Films on American Culture*. New York: William Morrow, 1977.

Walker, Alexander. *Stardom: The Hollywood Phenomenon*. New York: Stein and Day, 1970.

Weales, Gerald. *Canned Goods as Caviar: American Film Comedy of the 1930s*. Chicago: University of Chicago Press, 1985.

Wilkins, Joan Anderson. *Breaking the TV Habit*. New York: Charles Scribner's Sons, 1982.

Winn, Marie. *The Plug-In Drug: Television, Children and the Family*. Revised edition. New York: Penguin Books, 1985.

Yacowar, Maurice. *Loser Take All: The Comic Art of Woody Allen*. New expanded edition. New York: Continuum, 1991.

Index

Movie Index

Please note that the following movie titles appeared in this book's discussion of screen entertainment. Movies were cited as examples of poor-quality as well as high-quality film making. This is not a recommended viewing list.